THE *Birthday Cake* BOOK

Other books by Dede Wilson

Truffles

A Baker's Field Guide to Cupcakes

A Baker's Field Guide to Holiday Candy and Confections

Wedding Cakes You Can Make

A Baker's Field Guide to Chocolate Chip Cookies

A Baker's Field Guide to Christmas Cookies

The Wedding Cake Book

DEDE WILSON

THE *Birthday Cake* BOOK

75 RECIPES FOR CANDLE-WORTHY CREATIONS

Photographs by Melissa Punch

The Harvard Common Press ★ Boston, Massachusetts

The Harvard Common Press

535 Albany Street ★ Boston, Massachusetts 02118 ★ www.harvardcommonpress.com

Copyright © 2008 by Dede Wilson ★ Photographs copyright © 2008 by Melissa Punch

Printed in China

Printed on acid-free paper

Library of Congress Cataloging-in-Publication Data

Wilson, Dede.

The birthday cake book : 75 recipes for candle-worthy creations / Dede Wilson.

p. cm.

Includes index.

ISBN-13: 978-1-55832-381-0 (hardcover : alk. paper)

ISBN-13: 978-1-55832-382-7 (pbk. : alk. paper)

1. Birthday cakes. I. Title.

TX771.W468 2008

641.8'653--dc22

2008003498

Special bulk-order discounts are available on this and other Harvard Common Press books.
Companies and organizations may purchase books for premiums or resale, or may arrange a custom
edition, by contacting the Marketing Director at the address above.

Book design by Night & Day Design ★ Photographs by Melissa Punch
Food styling by Sara Neumeier ★ Prop styling by Lauren Ann Niles

2 4 6 8 10 9 7 5 3

Dedication

Happy Birthday to *you*!

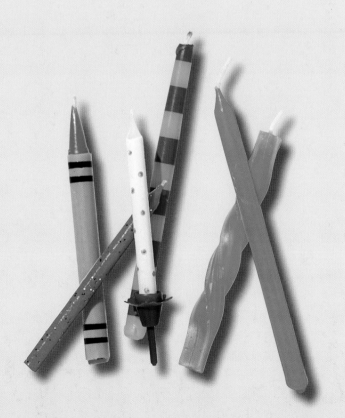

Acknowledgments

Thank you to the entire crew at The Harvard
Common Press.

A huge thank you to photographer Melissa Punch,
food stylist Sara Neumeier, assistant Matthew
Burdi, prop stylist Lauren Anne Niles, and Sharo,
our mascot.

Thank you to my agents, Maureen and Eric Lasher,
who are really extended family.

Thank you to Barbara Fairchild and everyone at
Bon Appétit magazine.

Thank you to Beryl's Cake Decorating and Pastry
Supplies, Crate and Barrel, Dinosaur Designs,
Meadowsweets, and Wilton Industries, Inc., for
providing items for the photographs.

Thank you to my very own personal support team.
Each of you is full of love and wisdom and I cherish
our friendships: Juanita Plimpton, Mary McNamara,
Pam Rys, and Marion Dussault.

And, as always, to my family—Ravenna, Freeman,
Forrester, and my life/work/love partner, David.

Contents

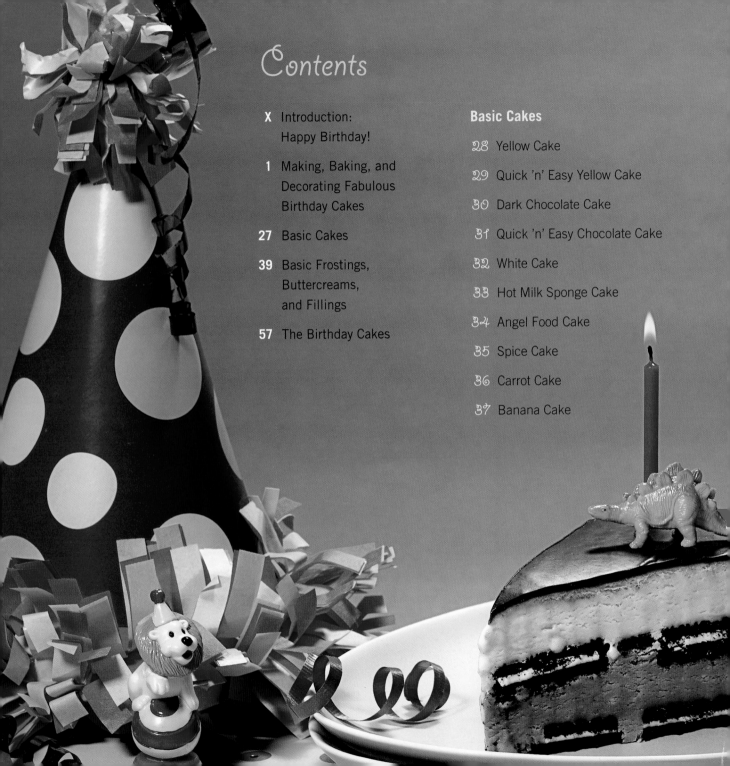

Basic Frostings, Buttercreams, and Fillings

The Birthday Cakes

Happy Birthday!

Someone out there is celebrating today, and I hope he or she is being treated to a fabulous birthday cake. Young, old, or in-between, everyone appreciates a celebration of this special day, especially when presented with a baked-from-scratch cake. Baking a cake for a cherished friend or family member is a personal way to show how much you care. I truly believe that a cake baked with love can nourish the soul and create warm memories. I have packed this book with more than 50 birthday cake recipes, accompanying frostings, and decorating ideas and have organized it to be as user-friendly as possible, so that you can achieve the birthday cake of your dreams. The combinations are endless.

What Makes a Cake a Birthday Cake?

While researching this book, I asked many people to recall their favorite birthday cakes; as expected, their responses were quite varied. Whether it's chocolate cake, yellow cake, cakes with citrus flavors, cakes with berries, ice cream cakes, or even cheesecakes, they are all here. It's clear that a birthday cake is whatever makes the birthday boy or girl happy—and involves candles. A layer cake presented on a platter is just a cake, but add some candles and that immediately signifies it is meant for someone's special day.

The other definitive aspect of a birthday cake is some sort of decoration. Remember the store-bought cakes you enjoyed as a child, and the arguments that erupted over who got the frosting roses? Decorations can be made from frosting, such as the afore-mentioned roses, and of course there is often personalized writing on the cake, but many people also have memories of tiny toys and ornaments or special birthday-candle holders handed down as family heirlooms. A plain cake becomes a birthday cake in the eye of the beholder when it is be-decked with frosting decorations, candy, toys, treats, or some other sort of decoration beyond what a cake usually has.

How to Use this Book

In the first chapter, "Making, Baking, and Decorating Fabulous Birthday Cakes," I guide you in choosing the perfect cake for your occasion. There's detailed information on ingredients, techniques, and equipment as well as baking, applying buttercream, frosting decorations, writing on cakes, candles—everything necessary to make the cakes taste great and look celebratory.

There are two ways to use this book. To create a cake à la carte, turn to the second and third chapters, "Basic Cakes" and "Basic, Frostings, Buttercreams, and Fillings," and mix and match whatever combinations you like. If your birthday celebrant wants a Yellow Cake with Fudgy Chocolate Frosting or a Dark Chocolate Cake with Fluffy Meringue Frosting, those classic recipes are found in those chapters.

If you prefer more guidance with specific recommendations, then go to "The Birthday Cakes." Here you will find cakes to suit any kind of birthday, be it for a child, a spouse, or a special

someone, a small gathering or large. These individual recipes have complete cake, filling, and frosting ideas ready for you to bake, such as the Beginner Baker's Birthday Cake, which can be made with absolutely no baking experience; the Office Birthday Cake, for when you need an easy-to-transport cake; and the Ice Cream Birthday Cake, which you assemble—no baking required. Some cakes are built upon the basics provided in earlier chapters. Others stand alone as singular sensations, such as the Luscious Lemon-Blueberry Meringue Cake, Sour Cream–White Chocolate Cheesecake with Raspberries, Coconut Rum Cake, or the Chocolate Extravaganza Birthday Cake—this last one for those who can never get enough chocolate.

I have written this book to help you bake memorable, delectable birthday cakes and I truly believe you will find "your" cake in these pages. Happy birthday to you all—may your special day be filled with moist cake and sweet frosting.

Dede

Making, Baking, and Decorating
Fabulous Birthday Cakes

Choosing what cake to make is your first step, and it's simply a matter of knowing the birthday person and the circumstances of the celebration. Consider three key elements: flavor, decoration, and setting.

Number one is flavor. Is she chocolate crazy or a lemon lover? Is carrot cake his all-time favorite? Maybe the recipient has mentioned that his beloved childhood cake contained coconut, or perhaps the birthday girl is allergic to nuts. Keep this information in mind when creating the cake, and the result will truly be meaningful.

Number two is how the cake is to be decorated, and this is where you can be especially creative. Two different people might like chocolate cake and vanilla frosting, but one might want deep-red frosting roses and the other a frosting tinted a favorite shade of green. To tailor a cake and its decoration specifically for the lucky recipient, consider the embellishments suggested in this chapter or work with things you know about the birthday person. Does he or she like cars? Dogs? Flowers? Then perch tiny toys on top of the cake. Is his or her favorite color red, yellow, or purple? Use that shade to tint either the frosting overall or just the decorative flourishes. Is he or she the kind of person who would appreciate lots of sprinkles and sparkles and fanfare? The craft and cake-decorating sources are full of choices. Or is your recipient a minimalist? A cake sporting a simple chocolate glaze would be perfect in this case. Whatever decorations you select should be chosen with the birthday person in mind.

Number three is setting. Is the cake for a young child's party or an adult gathering after dinner? Will the cake be served to four guests in the comfort of the home, or to 24 colleagues at the office? Does the cake require refrigeration—and if so, will it fit in the refrigerator? No matter what the occasion, there are many choices for the perfect cake.

Most of the cakes in this book are standard 8- or 9-inch layer cakes. Each one serves at least a dozen people, and if the crowd is smaller, guests will happily take home leftovers. There are also small cakes such as the Teeny Tiny Milk Chocolate–Orange Cake (page 144), geared toward diminutive parties of four to six, and cakes for larger groups such as The Big Birthday Cake (page 67) that serves up to 60 people.

The proper ingredients, equipment, and techniques are crucial to successful baking. Here's a rundown that will help you create the perfect cake.

Ingredients

Baking Powder and Baking Soda: Make sure both are fresh or their leavening power will be diminished. If they are kept in airtight containers, they will have a longer shelf life. Baking powder comes in such a container, but you might have to transfer baking soda. In general, baking soda will last indefinitely (if not exposed to moisture), but baking powder should be used within one year of purchase. The baking powder I prefer is double acting (such as Davis or Rumford brand), which means it reacts first when exposed to liquids in the batter (that's why it is so important to store it airtight) and then reacts again in the oven.

Butter: Use unsalted butter, since salt is added separately in the recipes and unsalted, sweet butter has better flavor for baked goods. To soften cold butter, I place unwrapped sticks of butter on a microwaveable plate and heat in the microwave with 10-second bursts on high power. You want to soften, not melt, the butter, so watch it carefully. Another solution is to grate cold butter on the largest holes of a box grater; the small pieces will warm up very quickly.

Chocolate: There are now many brands of chocolate to choose from, and they vary widely in flavor, texture, and overall quality. I sometimes make specific recommendations in the individual recipes, so be aware that a different chocolate will yield different results. This does not mean that you can't make substitutions based on your preferences, but the recipes were tested with specific chocolates and I want you to know which, so that you can get reliable results. In general, semisweet and bittersweet chocolates can be used interchangeably, but I find this to be most true with chocolates that are between 50 percent and 60 percent cacao content. (You will find the cacao content percentage on many chocolate labels. This percentage refers to the actual cacao mass content; the higher the percentage, the darker the chocolate.) Chocolates in the 70 percent range can be more temperamental when substituted in a recipe that was created with a chocolate that was in the 50 percent range, so only do this if you have time to experiment. In general, I like Scharffen Berger, Callebaut, and Ghirardelli unsweetened chocolate; Valrhona, Scharffen Berger, Merckens, and Ghirardelli bittersweet and semisweet chocolate; Valrhona and Callebaut milk chocolate; and Valrhona white chocolate.

Cocoa: Recipes specify natural or Dutch-processed cocoa, and they should not be substituted for one another, as they have different acidity levels and react differently in recipes. I prefer Scharffen Berger natural cocoa and Valrhona or Bensdorp Dutch-processed cocoa.

Confectioners' sugar: Frequently used in frostings, this white powdered sugar can compress during storage. A one-pound package equals approximately four cups. To measure accurately, sift the sugar into a bowl, and then use the dip-and-sweep method (described below under "Flour"). Manufacturers add a bit of cornstarch to the mixture to help prevent clumping, which in turn helps stabilize sweetened whipped cream when it is used as a frosting.

Eggs: All recipes use large eggs. Room-temperature eggs will incorporate more readily into butter and sugar during the creaming phase, which many of these cake recipes employ. Remove eggs from the refrigerator one hour before needed to bring them to room temperature. If you should forget, put the eggs in their shells in a bowl of warm, not hot, water for about five minutes, then proceed with recipe.

Extracts: Use pure vanilla and almond extracts. Nielsen-Massey is an excellent brand. I do not like or use lemon extract, as I find the flavor to be very artificial. I prefer fresh citrus juices and zests.

Flour: All-purpose flour (King Arthur unbleached) and cake flour (Pillsbury Softasilk) were used to test these recipes, and they do yield different results, so please do not substitute one for the other. Both are available nationwide. Also, make sure to purchase cake flour and not self-rising cake flour. All-purpose flours have between 10 and 12 percent protein and are made from hard wheat or a blend of hard and soft wheat. Cake flours have 6 to 8 percent protein and are made from soft wheat. The lower protein percentage yields a more tender crumb. Cake flour should be sifted before measuring as it clumps easily during storage. In a pinch, for every 1 cup of cake flour needed, you can take 1 cup all-purpose flour, remove 2 tablespoons, and replace with

2 tablespoons cornstarch.

Dry ingredients such as all-purpose flour, cake flour, confectioners' and granulated sugars, and cocoa are measured with the dip-and-sweep method. For cake flour, cocoa, and confectioners' sugar, sift first. For other dry ingredients, use a whisk to loosen up and aerate the ingredients in their canisters before measuring, as they settle upon storage. Then dip the correct size measuring spoon or cup into the ingredient and level it off with the back of a knife or an icing spatula. If you dip and sweep without sifting or aerating first, spoon the ingredient into the cup, or tap or shake down the cup, you will get a very different measurement and the cake will not bake properly.

Food Coloring: I call for colored pastes or gels, liquids, and powders. See individual recipes for specific items required. The liquid type can be found in the supermarket. The others can be found in craft or cake-decorating stores or purchased by mail order (see Resources, page 154).

Light and Dark Brown Sugars: Lightly pack brown sugar into dry measuring cups of the required size.

Milk, Cream Cheese, Sour Cream: Use full-fat varieties. Although low-fat versions might work, I tested these recipes with full-fat products and can vouch for the results. If you would like to experiment with low-fat dairy products, you certainly can, but do not substitute nonfat products, as they will not work in these recipes.

Nonstick Cooking Spray/Pan Coating: I use unflavored Pam to coat baking pans. I do not recommend the oil-flour combination sprays, as I find they leave a heavy residue on cakes.

Oil: Some of the recipes require a flavorless vegetable oil. Canola is a good choice, as is safflower.

Salt: Use table salt, as other salts will measure differently.

Sugar: The term "sugar" in the recipes refers to white granulated cane sugar. Measure sugar by dipping the measuring cup into the sugar canister and sweeping off any excess with the back of a knife or an icing spatula.

Equipment

Cake Decorating Turntable: I can't imagine decorating a cake without a turntable. It makes applying frosting so much easier and the results are professional looking. I use an Ateco turntable (see Resources, page 154), which has a heavy base that prevents it from moving during use and a smooth-turning, easy-to-clean metal surface for the cake. Al-though pricey, it is an investment that will last a lifetime. There are less expensive plastic lazy Susans, but they are lightweight and shift around on the work surface, making cake decorating difficult.

Cake Pans: This book is all about baking the very best cakes possible, and just as high-quality ingredients make a huge dif-ference, so do the cake pans. I experimented with the Yellow Cake (page 28) by dividing the batter between two cake pans of varying quality and then bak-ing them at the same time. One pan was Wilton's Decorator Preferred brand, which I always use for its sturdiness, even heat-ing, and reliability. The other was a thin, flimsy pan I bought at the supermarket. The cake in the supermarket pan peaked in the center and was overcooked

10 Tips for Successful Baking

1. Read each recipe thoroughly and follow it to the let-ter. Use only the ingredients listed in each recipe (no substitutions), measure them as specified, and use the appropriate equipment. For example, replacing a 9-inch pan with an 8-inch pan will not work.

2. Use high-quality measuring cups and spoons. My stainless-steel measuring equipment comes from Williams-Sonoma and The Baker's Catalogue. Cheap, poorly made measuring spoons and cups are often improperly calibrated, and that will wreak havoc with any recipe. Invest in high-quality equipment; it will last forever.

3. Use high-quality cake pans. The same batter baked in thin, flimsy cake pans can yield dramatically differ-ent results—and not for the better. Look for sturdy aluminum pans 1.0 to 1.5 mm thick. This thickness and material will give you uniformly baked cakes with even color and consistent texture. Straight sides at a 90-degree angle give the cake a clean shape, and rolled edges allow for an easy grip. Some companies even offer lifetime guarantees.

4. Use an oven thermometer to make sure that your oven is calibrated properly. Keep one in the oven at all times. These can be found in hardware and house-wares stores.

5. Do not overbake your cakes. The recipes give time cues, which are approximations, as well as visual cues. The visual cues are the most important. I usually suggest baking a cake until a wooden toothpick (or a wooden skewer for very deep cakes) inserted into the center of a layer shows a few moist crumbs when removed; don't wait for the toothpick to emerge com-

around the edges, and the cake's texture was rough and uneven. The cake in the Wilton pan had a level surface, a consistent overall color, and most important, a tender, even crumb throughout. The difference was dramatic. Invest in quality baking pans and you will have them forever. All of the cakes in this book were tested using Wilton pans. This is very important to note, as baking times in different pans can vary as much as 20 percent and the baking times suggested throughout the book refer to cakes baked in high-quality pans.

Cake Cardboards: Professional bakers transfer their baked layers to corrugated cardboard rounds, squares, or other shapes that are a generous ⅛ inch thick and pre-cut to the exact dimensions of the cake. The cardboard protects cakes from being squashed and misshapen during storage, and makes it easier to pick up cakes and move them around, especially when transferring them from a decorating turntable to a serving platter. My favorite reason for using cardboard is that the smooth edge of the cardboard provides a guide for the icing spatula when applying frosting. When I teach cake bak-

pletely clean, because residual heat continues to bake the cake even after it's removed from the oven.

6 Cool your pans on wire racks, which allow air circulation all around the cake. Once cooled to just warm, unmold the cakes onto the racks themselves, remove the parchment, if applicable, and cool thoroughly. (Exceptions such as angel food and chiffon cakes are noted in recipes.) Proper cooling helps the cake's texture be as good as it can be. To unmold, run an icing spatula around the edges between the cake and the pan to facilitate removal, if necessary.

7 Most of these cakes can be made a day before filling and frosting them. Place the layers on cardboards that are the same size as the cake pans, double-wrap each layer in plastic wrap, and store at room temperature. The cardboards protect the shape of the layers during storage. To fill and frost, remove the cardboard from all but the bottom cake layer.

8 Precut cardboards provide a smooth guide for your icing spatula when applying frosting. A turntable, cardboards in the same shape and diameter as the layers, and an icing spatula are the three most important tools for making professional-looking cakes. (See the Equipment section, above.) These recipes are written assuming you will use cardboards to support the cakes.

9 Follow the storage instructions in the individual recipes. If a cake is to be refrigerated, bring it to room temperature before serving (exceptions are noted). The butter in many of these cakes and frostings must soften to allow the best texture and flavors to come through.

10 Enjoy baking! Have fun!

ing I sound like a broken record, repeating that the three most important items for decorating a cake that looks professional are a turntable, icing spatula, and cardboards in the shape of the cake—but it's true! Don't try to cut your own, as the edges will be jagged and you need a smooth edge. Precut cardboards are inexpensive and can be purchased at cake-decorating and craft stores. Buy the same size and shape as the cake you are making—a 9-inch round cake requires a 9-inch round cardboard, and an 8-inch square cake requires an 8-inch square cardboard. If you are storing the cake layers for a period of time before assembling, use one cardboard for each cake layer to protect it.

Chocolate Chopper: Sometimes called a chocolate chipper in catalogues, this device looks like a heavy-duty fork with sharp tines. It makes quick work of chopping bulk chocolate into pieces suitable for melting (see Resources, page 154).

Icing Spatulas: A must for decorating cakes. Icing spatulas are not the same as the rubber spatulas used to scrape the cake batter into the pans. Icing spatulas have flat metal blades with smooth edges and rounded tips, and often have wood or plastic handles. They can be straight or offset, which means they have a bend or angle in them. They can range from a mere 5 inches long to over 14 inches. If you buy only one, buy an 8-inch straight-bladed icing spatula, which I find to be the most versatile. Some are stiff and some are flexible; I prefer a flexible version, but try out a couple and see what works best for you. Not only will you use icing spatulas to frost cakes, they are also great for slipping under cardboard rounds to aid in transferring the cake from the turntable to serving platter and to help release cakes from pans. Take care with the icing spatula blades, as any dent or chip along the edge will create a ripple in the icing.

Knives: Some recipes require the cake layers to be sliced in half horizontally. A sharp, thin, long-bladed knife with a straight edge gives the best results. Serrated knives work, but they dredge up crumbs, which are the bane of any cake decorator's existence. It also helps if the blade is longer than the diameter of the cake you are slicing.

Measuring Cups and Spoons: Believe it or not, measuring cups and spoons can vary tremendously, as some brands are not properly calibrated to industry standards. Measuring spoons can be off by as much as a factor of two! Imagine if half, or double, the proper amount of baking powder were added to a cake and you can see what mayhem would ensue. High-quality, accurate, sturdy measuring implements are a must. Williams-Sonoma and The Baker's Catalogue carry excellent ones (see Resources, page 154). If you bake frequently, the sets featuring odd-size cups (¾ cup, for example) and measuring spoons (½ tablespoon) are quite handy.

Microplane Zester: This tool is a sharp fine grater that allows you to grate citrus zests with

How to Make a Parchment Cone

Parchment cones are easy to make and come in handy when you do not want to wash out a pastry bag or don't have one handy. I always use a parchment cone, for example, when decorating with melted chocolate.

1 Start with a triangle cut from parchment paper. You should have two equal shorter sides and one longer side. The center of the long edge will form the point of the cone.

2 Hold the triangle with the long side along the top.

3 Take the top right corner and fold it down toward the left, curling it under itself and pulling it back toward the right, until the corner meets up with the point opposite the center of the long side. (See photo 1.)

4 Take the last extended corner and wrap it around the entire outside of the cone so that it meets up with the first two corners. Jiggle back and forth so that the fit is perfect and the point is tight. (See photo 2.)

5 Fold the section with the three corners outward to secure. (See photo 3.) The cone is ready to fill.

Never overfill the cone. Fill it up about halfway, then fold the open edge over itself several times to make a seal. Snip off the point with sharp scissors. For most chocolate work you need only a tiny opening; make a large opening prior to filling to use with tips. Discard the cone when you are finished.

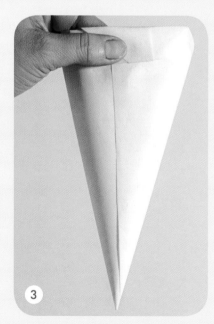

5 Tips for Frosting Cakes

1. Make sure the frosting is soft and spreadable. If it is just a little bit too cold or stiff, it will not apply smoothly.

2. Use a precut cardboard under the cake that is the same size and shape as the cake, to help guide the icing spatula when applying the crumb-coat and smooth final coating.

3. Keep the icing spatula gliding on top of the frosting. Do not let it touch the cake or you will bring crumbs up into the frosting.

4. Always make a thin crumb-coat to seal in crumbs. The final frosting layer will apply much more easily.

5. When using a pastry bag, fill the bag only halfway. Make sure that the frosting is soft and creamy enough to flow smoothly through the tip.

ease, without digging down into the bitter pith (see Resources, page 154). It creates a very fine, fluffy zest, and the measurements given for zests in the book were made using this tool.

Parchment Paper: Look for parchment in the supermarket near the aluminum foil and plastic wrap. Parchment has nonstick qualities that make it an excellent choice for lining pans. Waxed paper cannot be substituted. Parchment can also be formed into cones to fill with melted chocolate and soft icings to write on cakes.

Pastry Bags, Coupler, and Tips: Some decorations require the use of a pastry bag and decorating tips. The bags are cone shaped, and the reusable ones are made of either canvas or lightweight polyester, the latter of which clean particularly well and are the ones I use. You can also buy inexpensive disposable plastic bags. All bags come with their pointed end sealed, or almost sealed, so you need to snip off the end in order for the decorating tip or coupler to be slipped into the bag and

then emerge from the now-open end. Some larger decorating tips can slip directly into the bags; smaller tips require the coupler, which is a two-piece plastic device. The first piece, which has threads, slips into the bag and emerges out of the bag's end. The decorating tip is placed on it and the second coupler piece, a screw-top ring, is twisted down onto the first piece. The coupler holds the tip into place and also allows you to change tips easily. When the directions call for a pastry bag, coupler, and a specific tip, this means that the tip requires a coupler to be used. Where a coupler is not suggested, you should insert the tip, in this case a larger one (such as Wilton #2110 or Ateco #835), directly in the pastry bag (see Resources, page 154).

Pastry Brushes: My favorite invention of the past several years is the silicone pastry brush. Traditional pastry brushes are made of nylon or natural bristles, which often come loose and stick to the tops of baked goods. These old-school bristle brushes are difficult to clean and can't

be used interchangeably for a barbecue sauce and a dessert glaze, as they pick up flavors. The new silicone brushes have bristles that don't come loose, are dishwasher safe, and come completely clean of any residue. Look for one with very soft, thin, flexible bristles.

Rubber Spatulas: Not all "rubber" spatulas are created equal, and in fact, the best ones on the market these days are made from silicone (perhaps the tide is turning and bakers will start referring to them as "silicone spatulas"). Silicone is heat resistant,

which allows you to use the spatulas when cooking on the stovetop, and they clean easily with no residual flavors left behind. I have standard-size spatulas, extra-small ones for getting peanut butter out of the jar, and extra-large ones for folding egg whites into batter and working with large quantities of batter.

Sifter: Although you can buy an actual sifter for flour, cocoa, and confectioners' sugar, I use a fine-meshed metal strainer set over a bowl. The strainer is multipurpose and therefore probably already in the kitchen, and it works well.

Whisks: Whisks come in all shapes and sizes; some are stiff and some are quite flexible. I prefer them with some flexibility, making it easier to incorporate ingredients. Have a large balloon whisk and a small whisk at hand.

Baking Times

I give ranges for baking times, such as "Bake for 20 to 25 minutes," but I also include visual

cues for doneness. The times are simply a suggested range, so in the above example I would start assessing doneness at about 18 minutes. Do not be surprised if the cake isn't done until the 27-minute mark. This is because ovens can vary and heat retention of baking pans varies, as can temperature of ingredients. If the butter is 10 degrees colder than the last time you whipped up the cake, the baking time might indeed be longer. Most important are the visual and textural cues. Does a toothpick inserted in the center come out with a few crumbs clinging? Are the edges or top of the cake beginning to turn golden brown as mentioned in the recipe? These are the cues to pay close attention to, whether the cake has baked for 18, 22, or even 30 minutes.

Creating Multiple Layers

In some recipes I suggest slicing the baked cake layers in half horizontally to create additional layers before filling with frosting. To cut the layers in half, use a thin, sharp, straight-edged knife, preferably with a blade that is longer than the diameter of the cake. (Serrated blades encourage crumbs, which make applying frosting more difficult.) Place one cake layer on a cardboard of the same size, then place it on the turntable. Bring your eyes down to cake level so that you can assess the path of the knife as you cut; slice the cake evenly so that each half is the same height. Repeat with any additional layers. If you have spare cardboards, place each new layer on one; this will protect them as you move them around and assemble the cake.

How to Frost a Cake

There are many ways to apply frosting, some more casual than others. None is better; they are just different approaches that yield different results. Personally, I think a very homey approach, with swirls of thick frosting created and applied with a spoon, is a lovely way to finish off a birthday cake. Sometimes, however, you want a more polished look. With a few key techniques and pieces of equipment, you can frost a cake so it looks just like the ones in the bakery case.

Most frostings are very forgiving. Put it on, take it off, work it until it looks the way you want it to. If you are having problems applying it, chances are the frosting is too stiff and/or too cold. If the frosting is confectioners' sugar–based, add milk, teaspoon by teaspoon, until it is soft enough to spread more easily. If you are working with Italian Meringue Buttercream (page 42) and it is difficult to spread, see that recipe for instructions on heating it up to make it easier to work with.

For layer cakes, all the layers must be flat on top. If they are not, trim off any excess with a thin, long-bladed knife to create a level surface. When you put the topmost layer in place, it should be bottom side up. In other words, the part of the cake that was against the bottom of the pan during baking should now be facing up and creating the top of the cake. This is because the bottom will always be perfectly flat and will provide the best surface for the frosting on the top of the cake.

To fill and frost a layer cake, place one cardboard on the work surface. Dab a tablespoon of frosting in the middle of the cardboard, then place the bottom cake layer on top; the frosting will "glue" it to the cardboard. Lift the bottom cake layer on the cardboard to the turntable. With an icing spatula, apply a ¼-inch to ½-inch layer of frosting, ganache, lemon curd, etc., or a thin coating of jam, to the top. If using a filling different from the exterior frosting, make sure to stop ¼ inch short of the edges of the cake layers, so the filling will remain between the layers and not seep to the outside of the cake.

The first layer of frosting on the top and sides of the cakes is called a crumb-coat; it seals in any crumbs and allows for a smooth, final coat of frosting. Most frostings should be very smooth and slightly soft for easy spreading. To begin, apply about one cup of frosting to the top of the cake and very gently, with a light hand, spread the frosting over the top and to the edges of the cake. Rotate the turntable as needed to facilitate the process. Always keep the icing spatula gliding on top of the frosting, never allowing it to touch the cake itself, or the spatula will pick up cake crumbs. The goal is to create a thin veneer of frosting, just enough to seal in the crumbs. At this point, there will be a layer of frosting so thin that you can still see the cake beneath.

With the spatula, push any excess frosting onto the sides of the cake and apply more frosting to the sides. This is where the icing spatula and cardboard are going to come into play. Place the side edge of the icing spatula (spatula facing down, handle up) against the cake and edge of cardboard. Experiment with the angle of the spatula; it might be almost flat against the cake. Nestle the tip of the spatula against the cardboard and hold it still. Now rotate the turntable, applying inward pressure toward the cardboard to keep the spatula in place. The turntable moves; the spatula does not. As the table turns, the edge of the spatula will create a smooth surface of frosting. Once the cake is completely covered with this veneer of frosting, it is helpful to chill the crumb-coat until it is very firm to the touch. If using Italian Meringue Buttercream, it is imperative to chill the cake at this point until it is firm enough so that when you touch it, your fingertip does not come away with any buttercream attached. This can take an hour or more.

Applying the final layer of frosting is approached in the same manner, but with a few important differences. The crumb-coat will make this final coat go on much easier. This time, you are aiming for a thicker coating and, if you are going for a polished look, smooth surfaces and a sharp angle on the top edge of the cake. When you think you are done, bring your eyes down to cake level and spin the turntable. The cake might not be level across the top, and spinning it around will bring up any unevenness for you to see. Simply remove icing where it is too high or add icing where it is too low.

To create a more homespun look, apply the icing in a carefree manner, using the back of a spoon or the tip of the icing spatula to make whirls and swirls. Or apply a fairly smooth layer of frosting on tops and sides of the cake, and then press chopped nuts or cake crumbs onto the sides. This trick makes a cake look very polished, without your having to worry about making the frosting smooth.

Basic Frosting Decorations Using a Pastry Bag

You will need a pastry bag, couplers, and decorating tips. I use a 16-inch bag and a coupler, which allows for easy changing of tips, so I can make roses and contrasting borders easily on the same cake. When pastry bags are new, their narrow openings are too small to fit a coupler; they have to be cut to fit. Cut just so the coupler's threads are showing through the newly cut opening. This will allow the cap that comes with the coupler to screw on tightly after the tip is put into place on the coupler.

Choose a tip as specified in the instructions that follow. (When there is a range of numbers presented for tips, such as Ateco star tips #16 to #22, they are all the same shape, but the smaller the number, the smaller the tip.) Place the tip on the coupler and screw the coupler ring into place. Fill the bag about halfway with soft frosting. Twist the top of the bag closed, firmly against the frosting, which should be pressed down toward the tip end of the bag. Hold the bag gently with one hand down near the tip (this will be your guiding hand) and use your other hand to hold the twisted part closed tightly against the frosting; this hand will press down, applying pressure on the frosting, encouraging it to move toward and out of the tip.

Practice does help! Fill a bag with frosting and practice on an overturned cake pan so you can scrape up the frosting and keep practicing. Know that whatever tip you are using, the slightest change in angle of tip and bag will produce a different result. Varying pressure will also alter the look of what comes out of the tip, so practice, practice, practice.

These are some techniques for creating basic frosting decorations:
Writing: If you want to use a pastry bag and tip to write "Happy Birthday" and/or a name on a cake, use Ateco or Wilton tips #2 to #6, which are small plain round tips. I find tips smaller than #2 difficult to use, and larger tips make the writing too big. Press the frosting out of the tip and write in script or print.

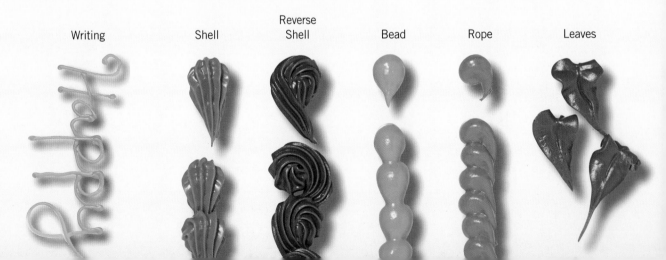

Writing   Shell   Reverse Shell   Bead   Rope   Leaves

Either go freeform or use a toothpick to poke pin dots onto the frosting first to form the letters as you desire.

Shells and Reverse Shells: Use Ateco tips #16 to #22 or Wilton tips #13 to #22, which are all open star tips. Hold the bag at a 45-degree angle to the cake and just slightly above the surface. Press the frosting out of the bag and allow it to accumulate at the starting point just enough so that it fans out on either side of the tip and builds up. The frosting will build up and contact the tip itself, at which point gradually release the pressure and move the tip forward and away from the start point, as you also bring it down toward the surface. Gradually release all pressure and pull the tip away. The first shell is completed. This technique makes a symmetrical shell; you can angle the bag and pipe the shell so that it lies on its side and shows more of an inner swirl. To make a shell border, begin the next shell right over the tail end of the first one. You can make elongated tails for thin, elegant shell shapes or small (or no) tails for shells that are plump and close together. A reverse shell is a chain of shells, lying on their side, alternating the direction of every other swirl.

Beads and Beaded Borders: Use Ateco or Wilton tips #6 to #12, which are plain round tips.

For individual beads, hold the bag vertically just above the cake surface. Squeeze out a small amount of frosting, releasing pressure when the "bead" is the size you desire. By quickly pulling the bag away to the side, if you do the movement correctly, the end of the tip will clip off any point that might have developed on the top of the bead. This will take some practice. Pipe out little balls of frosting right next to one another, creating a beaded look, to form a border. You can also pipe single beads randomly.

Rope Border: Use Ateco tips #8 to #12 or Wilton tips #6 to #12. These round tips can create a border that looks like a twisted rope. Begin by holding the bag at approximately a 45-degree angle to the cake surface. With even pressure, pipe an S shape. Release pressure. Insert the tip under the bottom curve and pipe the next S. Repeat to make a continuous "rope."

Leaves and Leaf Borders: Ateco tips #65 to #70 and

Rosette	Swirled Rosette	Flower Buds	Drop Flowers

Wilton tips #65 to #69 make a traditional-looking leaf, and Ateco tips #349, #350, and #352 and Wilton tip #352 make a more streamlined, contemporary-looking leaf. Leaves can accent flowers or be used alone. Create a neat leaf border by having the leaves overlap symmetrically, or pipe them at an angle to one another: one going to the right, the next to the left. For a leaf border, the leaves are usually piped facing the same general direction, whether they are neatly arranged or angled. Hold the pastry bag at approximately a 45-degree angle to the cake surface. Squeeze gently to build up the base of the leaf, while simultaneously lifting up the tip slightly, then squeeze downward and away from the base while lessening pressure. As you pull the tip away, the leaf should form a point. If it does not, it will leave a double "tail." Simply pinch those two points together to make a neat single point (fingers lightly moistened with water work best).

Rosettes: Use Ateco tips #16 to #22 or Wilton tips #13 to #22 for everything from simple rosettes to swirled rosettes. For simple ones, hold the bag vertically just above the cake surface. Squeeze out a small amount of frosting, releasing pressure when the rosette is the desired size and lifting the bag up and away. For swirled rosettes, start as a simple rosette but rotate the bag in a tight 360-degree motion, then release the pressure and pull up and away. You can make individual rosettes or pipe them next to one another to create a border.

Basketweave: To create the basketweave pattern, use an Ateco tip or Wilton tips #8, #10, or #11. You can also use tips #46 to #48 for a different basketweave look. For any of these tips, the technique is the same. Pipe one vertical bar on the cake's side spanning the entire height of the cake. Pipe horizontal bars across the first vertical bar, spaced apart so that subsequent bars can fit in between (in other words, the width of one bar). Make the horizontal bars about 1 inch long. Pipe another vertical bar over the ends of the horizontal bars. Fill in the open spaces with more horizontal bars, tucking the ends as neatly as possible under the prior vertical bars. Continue the pattern around the entire circumference of the cake.

Roses: Place a dab of icing on a flower nail and top with a small square of parchment. Use Ateco or Wilton round tips #8 to #12 for the centers and tips #101 to #104 for the petals. (Tips #8 and #104 were used in the photos above.) Use the round tip to pipe a center cone onto the flower nail, as shown in photo 1. Using tip #104, hold the bag so that the narrow end is facing up and is slightly tilted in toward the

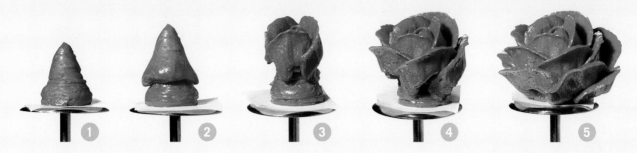

center. Pipe your rose center by wrapping a strip of buttercream around the center cone, twirling the flower nail as you go. This is the center of the rose, as shown in photo 2. To create the first row of three petals, shown in photo 3, hold the bag so the narrow end of the tip is still facing up and pipe in a slight arching motion, starting low, arching up in a rounded motion and then coming down, twirling the nail as you go; this is one petal. Two more petals, each one slightly overlapping, create the remainder of the row. Subsequent rows, depicted in photos 4 and 5, show more petals, each one piped slightly overlapping the one before. Make the rose as small or as large as you like. Carefully remove the parchment paper and rose from the flower nail using a small offset spatula; place on a tray. Refrigerate until the rose is firm enough to be safely transferred to the cake.

Flower Buds: Use Ateco or Wilton tips #101 to #104 to make buds directly on the cake. Practice on a plate before you pipe on the cake. Hold the bag at a 45-degree angle to the cake surface with the wide end of the tip toward the bottom and touching the cake surface. Squeeze gently and, at the same time, slightly lift the tip off of the surface; the frosting will flow out in a petal shape. Ease up on the pressure and bring the tip back down to the surface, release the pressure and pull down and away. This is the center petal. Make additional petals to the left and right of the first petal in the same manner. Leaves, made with the leaf tips, can be piped to cover the base of the flower and provide a more realistic look.

Drop Flowers: Wilton tips #129 (see frosting pictured on page 13) and #190 (both with a coupler), #1B, #2D, and #2F (used directly in the bag with no coupler) are my favorites for this kind of flower; they are used in conjunction with small round tips such as Wilton #2 or #3 for the centers, which can be in the same color or a contrasting one. Using tips #129, #190, #1B, #2D, or #2F, hold the bag vertically above the cake, with your wrist turned inward toward you (for right-handed folks, your knuckles will be facing the 9 o'clock position). Just touching the surface, begin to slowly press frosting out of the bag as you simultaneously turn your wrist, ending at the 12 o'clock position. Gently pull the bag up and away. You can also press out frosting without the twisting action. Use a small round tip to add a dot-shaped center.

More Birthday Cake Decorations

Frosting roses are classic, but don't overlook the other options available. Cake-decorating stores, craft stores, and the candy aisle are filled with a great selection of suitable decorations, some edible, some not. Mail-order sources are invaluable as well. You can find everything from marzipan animals and vegetables to candy that looks like pebbles to fruit, flowers, and leaves to sparkly sugars and glitter in every color of the rainbow and even tiny toys that are food safe. Your own home might be a treasure trove as well. Perhaps there is a small toy or objet d'art that is meaningful to the birthday person. I once crowned a cake with a porcelain Beatrix Potter mouse that the birthday girl had always treasured; it is personal touches such as this that will make each and every cake unique.

Writing on Cakes

Often you will want to write "Happy Birthday," perhaps in conjunction with a name, on top of the cake. The writing can be as simple or as fancy as you like. Smooth, soft frosting in a contrasting color or melted chocolate are great. If the cake is covered with white frosting, tint the writing frosting to any color of your choice with food coloring. Whipped cream can

Red Candy Hearts

Silver Dragées

Candy Rocks

Candy Flowers

be used as well, but it works best on dark-colored cakes. Melted chocolate is a good choice, as long as it has cooled enough to be slightly thick and not too runny, or it will flow too quickly through the decorating tip or parchment cone. You can use white, milk, or dark chocolate. Parchment cones are my choice when using chocolate; there are photos on page 7 that show how to make one. Fill the cone half to two-thirds of the way and snip a very small hole in the tip. You can always enlarge the hole if needed.

Look up font styles on the Internet or in books and photocopy them, making them larger or smaller as needed. Block style, script, bold, or delicate—there are thousands to choose from. Place a piece of parchment over the page with the letters—you will be able to see through it—and practice with frosting on the parchment. (You can also approach the lettering freeform, as you do when writing by hand, and the look will be unique to you.) Then practice writing on the bottom of the cake pan, since it is the exact dimension of the cake. That way, you can figure out how to make the lettering the appropriate size for the cake. (The biggest mistakes people make are writing too large and not starting far enough to the

Gumdrops

Multicolored
Round Dragées

Chocolate
Sprinkles

Crystallized
Flowers

Candy
Stars

left on the cake and running out of room.) Use a bit of the frosting, or practice with softened vegetable shortening—just stir it in a bowl before filling a pastry bag with a tip. Ease up on the pressure you apply to the pastry bag or cone when you come to the part of a letter where you go over it twice, or the result will be thick and ungainly. Even if the writing comes out a bit wobbly, don't worry. There is an ineffable charm to all homemade cakes and the efforts will show how much you care.

Candles Make It a Birthday Cake

Candles are not to be overlooked—they are a must-have to signify the birthday celebration, and candles can be as personal and varied as the cake. Beyond the classic short spiral ones found in supermarkets, there are slender elegant candles that are almost 7 inches in length, candles that glow in the dark, trick candles that relight when blown out, candles shaped like numbers and letters, and themed candles in the shape of soccer players, dinosaurs, flowers, and so on. Wilton has

an enormous selection, and I also always check dollar stores and gift shops to keep a supply on hand. Babykakes, Inc. and 100 Candles are two mail-order companies that have a great assortment, from candles that look like sea horses and ballerinas to ones that resemble monarch butterflies and pansies.

Candles can be put on directly on the cake or in decorative candleholders. Simple plastic holders can be found in supermarkets. Reusable silver, pewter, or ceramic sets of birthday-cake candleholders can be purchased new, or vintage sets are available

from online auctions. They usually come in sets of six, in themes such as Peter Rabbit, Teddy bears, and more. These candleholders are exceptional baby-shower gifts, and can be passed down to the next generation. See the Resources section, page 154.

Other creative ideas include using LifeSavers candies to hold candles (choosing a candy flavor to complement the cake, of course); caramels, gumdrops, and peppermint patties work, too. Instructions for making gumdrop candleholders are given below. Take a walk down the candy aisle and look for new ideas.

Gumdrop Flower Candleholders

Makes 12

½ **cup sugar**

Aluminum foil

12 large gumdrops, 1¼ inches across the bottom

12 small gumdrops, ¾ inch across the bottom

Bamboo or metal skewer

1. Place the sugar in a small bowl; set aside.
2. Put a small piece (about 6 × 6 inches) of aluminum foil on a work surface and place large gumdrop on top. Place another piece of foil on top, and using your palm to press, flatten out the gumdrop. It should now be a flat disc about 2 inches across. Dip the flattened gumdrop in the sugar to reduce stickiness.
3. Use small knife to make six equally spaced cuts all the way around the circle going in about ½ inch from edge (this creates the petals).
4. Dip your fingertips in the sugar, grab each petal and give it a slight twist while also smoothing and rounding out the edges. Repeat with small gumdrops.
5. To assemble, place a small gumdrop on top of the large gumdrop to create a three-dimensional flower. Use a skewer to make a hole through the center of both gum-drops. Place flowers on cake and then insert the candles through the hole and into the cake. (See photo at left.)

NOTE: *Gumdrop flowers can be stored at room temperature in an airtight container for up to 1 month.*

Crystallized Flowers

These are featured on the Liqueured-Up Layer Cake with Vanilla Buttercream and Crystallized Flowers (page 115), but crystallized flowers can embellish any number of the cakes, so I have included this recipe for making your own. If you prefer, you can purchase exquisite crystallized flowers from Meadowsweets (see Resources, page 154). It is best to make a large quantity at a time because if dried and stored properly, they can last for up to one month. They must be kept dry in an airtight container.

Crystallized Flowers

Makes 30 flowers

30 small edible flowers (1- to 2-inch diameter) such as pansies, violets, Johnny-jump-ups, small roses, or rose petals that have not been sprayed

2 cups superfine sugar

2 large egg whites

Tweezers

Small soft artist's brush

1. Make sure the flowers are dry, and choose specimens without any bruises, nicks, or cuts.
2. Place the sugar in a small bowl.
3. Whisk the egg whites until frothy in another small bowl.
4. Hold the base of one flower at a time with tweezers or your fingertips. Use a brush to apply a thin, even coat of egg white to all of the petal surfaces.
5. Immediately hold the flower over the bowl of sugar, and using a teaspoon, scoop up and

sprinkle sugar evenly over the flower so it sticks. Gently shake the flower to remove excess sugar.

6. Place the flower on a wire rack to dry. Repeat with the other flowers. Place the rack of flowers in a warm, dry location (inside an unlit gas oven with a pilot light is perfect, if you have one). Let the flowers dry thoroughly, at least overnight or until completely dry and crisp.

7. Store in single layers in air-tight containers. Do not layer them. Even if separated by parchment, the petals can be crushed.

Candy Plastic Roses, Leaves, and Tendrils

Refer to the Candy Plastic recipe on page 55. It must have firmed up enough to roll out. Cut off about a 4-inch square piece at a time and knead until soft. If it is very hard, hold it in your palms for a minute to warm it up. You will need special gum-paste cutters in the shape of rose petals—they come in a set of several sizes and are not expensive—as well as a set of rose leaf cutters and a veining mat. This last item transfers a vein pattern to the leaves for a very realistic look. I also use a small silicone rolling pin and smooth board, all of which can be found at well-stocked cake-decorating stores or ordered from Beryl's (see Resources, page 154).

Lightly dust a cutting board with confectioners' sugar. Roll out the candy plastic to a thickness of ⅛ inch.

For roses: Cut out four petals from the plastic for every small, tight rose using the same size rose-petal cutter. Cut out seven to ten petals for larger roses. Use the rolling pin to thin out the tops of the petals.

To form the center of the rose, take one petal and hold the center top of the petal between your left index finger and thumb. Take your right hand and gently but tightly roll the upper right part of the petal diagonally toward the middle. The top will become the center's tip and should be tighter and narrower. When you get to the middle, remove your thumb and finger and continue rolling. (Reverse directions if you are left

handed.) You will have a cone-shaped petal that will form the center of the rose. At this point you have a choice as to the way to proceed, and the decision will depend on what feels easiest to you. You can either affix the base of the rose's center to the board, or you can work up in the air, between your two hands. Try both ways to see which works better for you.

Gently pinch the bottoms of all of the remaining petals, making them into a curved cup shape. Then gently bend the top edges back, forming a tight outward furl. Asymmetry is encouraged, as it is most realistic.

Place a petal against the cone base, pinched end down. Flatten one side against the cone, leaving the other side open and away from the cone. Place one edge of the second petal in the middle of the first petal and flatten the remaining portion of the second petal against the center. The third petal will begin in the center of the second petal and then be tucked under the first. These three petals formed around the center create a small rosebud. You may add additional petals, each beginning in the middle of the one underneath, to create as large a rose as you like. Experiment with keeping the petals tight against the center for a more closed rosebud look, or for a full-blown rose, loosen the petals and unfurl them a bit. You can manipulate and mold the petals once they are in place.

At this point the base of the rose will be thick. If the rose is attached to the board, release it from the work surface with a small offset icing spatula. Trim any excess plastic from the base with a sharp paring knife. You want to form the base into a reverse cone shape. This end will be nestled into the frosting and under the candy leaves, so it doesn't have to be perfect. When you are done, use a soft brush to dust off any extra confectioners' sugar.

Roses can be stored in a single layer in an airtight container in a cool, dry place for up to one month.

For leaves: Leaves should be made right before you place them on a cake so that they remain pliable (they dry upon storage). This way you can bend and drape them gently so that they look more realistic.

Cut out leaf shapes with cutters. Remove excess plastic from around the leaf shapes, just as when making cut-out cookies. Loosen the leaves from the board with a small offset icing spatula. Align and press the leaves against the veining mat to transfer the vein pattern onto them.

For tendrils: Tendrils should also be made right before you use them. Simply take a small portion of plastic and roll it into long, thin ropes that taper at the ends (see photo); ropes ranging from 6 to 10 inches are a good length, with widths varying according to the size of the roses. Place them directly on cake, tucking one end under the roses and leaves.

For instructions on gilding candy roses, leaves, and tendrils, see the Gilded Candy Roses Birthday Cake, page 101.

Storing Birthday Cakes

Once you have made your birthday creation, it makes sense to pay attention to the storage and serving instructions in the individual recipes, as these can greatly affect the final quality of your cake when it is presented. Some birthday cakes, such as cheesecakes, cakes with whipped cream, or ice cream cakes, require refrigeration (or freezing) and are served cold. Many of the cakes, however, are covered with confectioners' sugar–based frostings, in which case they can be stored at room temperature. Those filled and decorated with Italian Meringue Buttercream or Cream Cheese Frosting need refrigeration but are brought to room temperature before serving. There is so much butter in some of the cakes and buttercreams that refrigeration will leave both components quite firm. Bringing the cake to room temperature, in this case, will result in the best texture and flavor.

The best way to store the cake is on a plate or platter, under a cake dome; many of these are sold in sets. They are available in glass, simple or ornate ceramic, and even plastic (see Resources, page 154), which I happen to like, as these are often also airtight. Used either for room temperature or refrigerated storage, they protect the cake from circulating air (which can be drying), shield the cakes from dust and odors, and are typically high and wide enough not to touch the frosting, thereby allowing the cake to remain as pretty as when freshly decorated. I highly recommend buying one.

Freezing Cakes, Fillings, Frostings, and Buttercreams

There is nothing like a freshly baked cake. However, we all have busy lives, and those birthdays seem to come up yearly like clockwork—and not always on a convenient day. There are many components—cakes, fillings, and frostings—that can be made ahead, individually frozen, and then put together as close to serving time as possible. Below are lists of the cakes, fillings, and frostings from this book that can be successfully frozen, making it easy for you to plan ahead.

Freezing Cake Layers

Cake layers must be protected from freezer burn and from being crushed during freezer storage. Cardboards that are the same size as the cake will protect the shape of the cake. Many layers of plastic wrap and zipper-top plastic bags protect from freezer burn, as well as shield the cake from picking up off-flavors. Here are my techniques:

- Make sure the cake layers are completely cooled.
- Place every cake layer on a cardboard of the same size.
- Double-wrap each layer in plastic wrap.
- If there's room in the freezer and/or pans to spare, slip the cake into a cake pan (sometimes you need a slightly larger pan) for protection.
- If the cake fits, slip into a zipper-top plastic bag, remove the air, and seal.
- Make sure the cake does not get crushed in the freezer. Do

not place anything on top of the layers.

- Freeze cake for up to one month.
- Defrost the cake overnight in the refrigerator.

Basic cake layers that can be frozen without filling or frosting:
- Yellow Cake
- Quick 'n' Easy Yellow Cake
- Dark Chocolate Cake
- Quick 'n' Easy Chocolate Cake
- White Cake
- Carrot Cake
- Banana Cake
- Spice Cake

Other cakes and cake layers that can be frozen without filling or frosting:
- Hummingbird Cake (freeze in pan, if possible)
- Tropical Carrot Cake
- Sour Cream–White Chocolate Cheesecake with Raspberries
- PB.C.B. Cake
- Orange Chiffon Cake
- Coco-licious Cake
- Applesauce-Raisin-Walnut Spice Cake
- Amaretto-Chocolate Cheesecake
- The Office Birthday Cake
- Red Velvet Cake
- Heart of Gold Chocolate Raspberry Cake
- Teeny Tiny Milk Chocolate–Orange Cake
- Chocolate Almond Apricot Cake
- German Chocolate Cake
- The Birthday Cake You Can Mail

Freezing Fillings, Frostings, and Buttercreams

Fillings and frostings can be successfully frozen. Follow these tips for best results:
- Prepare the filling or frosting and make sure it is cooled and/or whipped to its full capacity.
- Scrape it into a properly sized airtight container with just a little headroom.
- Seal and freeze for up to one month.
- Defrost overnight in the refrigerator.
- Bring to room temperature before using.

Here are the fillings and frostings that can be successfully made ahead and frozen. Any not mentioned will suffer if frozen, so don't waste your time or ingredients.

- Italian Meringue Buttercream—all variations. Must be rebeaten until smooth after defrosting.
- Rich Egg Yolk Buttercream—all variations. Must be rebeaten until smooth after defrosting.
- Chocolate Ganache Glaze and Frosting. May be used at room temperature as a spreadable frosting. Remelt if using as a glaze.

Freezing Whole Cakes

Both of the cheesecakes in the book can be successfully frozen without their frostings for up to one month. Follow the instructions for Freezing Cake Layers above. Defrost the cheesecake in the refrigerator overnight, then frost and decorate the cake the day it will be served. Once frosted and decorated, refrigerate the cheesecake until serving time.

The Ice Cream Birthday Cake, of course, must be stored in your freezer. It just needs to sit at room temperature for a few minutes to soften slightly before serving.

I do not like to freeze whole frosted and decorated layer cakes. Instead, if necessary, you can freeze any of the freezer-approved cakes listed above with an initial crumb-coat of freezer-approved frostings (ditto), along with any freezer-approved fillings (also listed above). Once the crumb-coat is applied, chill the cake well, then wrap and freeze for up to one month as described above. Once it has defrosted overnight in the refrigerator, you can frost and decorate it the day of serving. This is the best way to bring a cake to the table that tastes as fresh as possible, while still taking advantage of do-ahead frozen convenience. By assembling the cake through the crumb-coat stage, you have not only done most of the work ahead of time, you've sealed in much of the moistness that might be lost in the freezer. The crumb-coat also protects the cake against absorbing odors. After the cake is defrosted and the final frosting applied, it will look and taste very fresh indeed.

Basic Cakes

These are the cake recipes that I turn to again and again. You will find

them used in more than one cake within the "Birthday Cakes" chapter, but

each time, they will be put together in a new way, creating a unique birthday

cake. A good example of this is The Office Birthday Cake. It starts with

the basic Carrot Cake found in this chapter, but to please the office hordes

I have jazzed it up with extra dried fruit and nuts and suggested some

specific decoration details. In this spirit I invite you to take these basic

recipes and make them your own.

Yellow Cake

Every baker should have a recipe for a basic yellow cake like this one. Its buttery flavor and moist texture make it the most versatile cake in the book. It has less sugar than most traditional yellow cakes, yielding a more delicate crumb. The eggs must be at room temperature, or they will not incorporate well into the butter. Any Italian Meringue Buttercream variation (page 42) or Confectioners' Sugar Frosting (page 40) works well with this cake, as does Caramel Frosting (page 51) or Fudgy Chocolate Frosting (page 47).

Makes two 9 x 2-inch round layers

3 cups sifted cake flour

1 tablespoon baking powder

¼ teaspoon salt

1 cup (2 sticks) unsalted butter, at room temperature, cut into small pieces

1½ cups sugar

1 teaspoon vanilla extract

4 large eggs, at room temperature

1 cup whole milk, at room temperature

1. Position a rack in the middle of the oven. Preheat the oven to 350°F. Coat the insides of two 9 × 2-inch round cake pans with nonstick cooking spray, line the bottoms with parchment rounds, then the spray the parchment.

2. Whisk together the flour, baking powder, and salt in a medium-size bowl to combine and aerate; set aside.

3. Beat the butter until creamy, about 2 minutes, with an electric mixer on medium-high speed. Add the sugar gradually and beat until very light and fluffy, about 3 minutes, scraping down bowl once or twice. Beat in vanilla.

4. Beat in the eggs one at a time, scraping down after each addition and allowing each egg to be absorbed before continuing. Add the flour mixture in three additions, alternately with the milk, while beating on low speed. Begin and end with the flour, and beat briefly until smooth. Divide the batter evenly between the pans and smooth the tops with an offset spatula.

5. Bake for 20 to 25 minutes, or until a toothpick inserted into the layers shows a few moist crumbs when removed. The layers will be tinged light golden brown around the edges and top and will have begun to come away from the sides of the pans.

6. Cool the pans on wire racks for 8 to 10 minutes. Unmold, peel off the parchment, and place the layers directly on the racks to cool completely. The layers are ready to fill and frost. Alternatively, place the cooled layers on cardboard rounds and double-wrap in plastic wrap; store at room temperature, and assemble and serve within 24 hours.

Quick 'n' Easy Yellow Cake

When you need a last-minute cake, here's one that goes together quickly. The ingredients are similar to the Yellow Cake, but the technique is different. For this cake, the butter is melted and then the wet and dry mixtures are combined. The only difference in the end is that with this recipe, each baked layer loses about ⅛ inch in height. The textures are near identical and the flavors equally buttery and delicious. Any Italian Meringue Buttercream variation (page 42) or Confectioners' Sugar Frosting (page 40) works well with this cake, as does Caramel Frosting (page 51) or Fudgy Chocolate Frosting (page 47).

Makes two 9 x 2-inch round layers

3 cups sifted cake flour

1½ cups sugar

1 tablespoon baking powder

¼ teaspoon salt

4 large eggs, at room temperature

1 cup whole milk, at room temperature

1 cup (2 sticks) unsalted butter, melted and cooled to warm

1 teaspoon vanilla extract

1. Position a rack in the middle of the oven. Preheat the oven to 350°F. Coat the insides of two 9 × 2-inch round cake pans with nonstick cooking spray, line the bottoms with parchment rounds, then spray the parchment.

2. Whisk together the flour, sugar, baking powder, and salt in a large bowl to combine and aerate; set aside.

3. Whisk the eggs and milk together in a medium-size bowl until thoroughly combined. Whisk in the melted butter and vanilla.

4. Pour the wet ingredients over the dry ones and whisk until combined. Divide the batter evenly between the pans.

5. Bake for 20 to 25 minutes, or until a toothpick inserted into the layers shows a few moist crumbs when removed. The cake might just begin to brown along the edges.

6. Cool pans on wire racks for 8 to 10 minutes. Unmold, peel off the parchment, and place the layers directly on the racks to cool completely. The layers are ready to fill and frost. Alternatively, place the cooled layers on cardboard rounds and double-wrap in plastic wrap; store at room temperature, and assemble and serve within 24 hours.

Dark Chocolate Cake

If your birthday boy or girl, guy or gal, loves chocolate cake, look no further. This one is moist and dark with a soft crumb and will satisfy a chocolate craving; pair with Fluffy Meringue Frosting (page 41), Fudgy Chocolate Frosting (page 47), Confectioners' Sugar Frosting (page 40), or pretty much any flavor variation of Italian Meringue Buttercream (page 42). Make sure to use Dutch-processed cocoa for this cake; I like Bensdorp and Valrhona brands.

Makes two 9 x 2-inch round layers

2 cups sifted cake flour

1 teaspoon baking soda

¼ teaspoon salt

⅔ cup sifted Dutch-processed cocoa

⅔ cup hot tap water

⅔ cup whole milk, at room temperature

10 tablespoons (1¼ sticks) unsalted butter, at room temperature, cut into small pieces

1¾ cups sugar

1 teaspoon vanilla extract

3 large eggs, at room temperature

1. Position a rack in the middle of the oven. Preheat the oven to 350°F. Coat the insides of two 9 × 2-inch round cake pans with nonstick cooking spray, line the bottoms with parchment rounds, then spray the parchment.

2. Whisk together the flour, baking soda, and salt in a medium-size bowl to combine and aerate; set aside. Whisk together the cocoa and hot water in a small bowl until smooth. Whisk in the milk; set aside.

3. Beat the butter until creamy, about 2 minutes, with an electric mixer on medium-high speed. Add the sugar gradually and beat until very light and fluffy, about 3 minutes, scraping down the bowl once or twice. Beat in the vanilla.

4. Beat in the eggs one at a time, scraping down after each addition and allowing each egg to be absorbed before continuing. Add the flour mixture in three additions, alternately with the cocoa mixture, while beating on low speed. Begin and end with the flour, and beat briefly until smooth. Divide the batter evenly between the pans and smooth the tops with an offset spatula.

5. Bake for 30 to 35 minutes, or until a toothpick inserted into the layers shows a few moist crumbs when removed.

6. Cool the pans on wire racks for 8 to 10 minutes. Unmold, peel off the parchment, and place the layers directly on the racks to cool completely. The layers are ready to fill and frost. Alternatively, place the cooled layers on cardboard rounds and double-wrap in plastic wrap; store at room temperature, and assemble and serve within 24 hours.

Quick 'n' Easy Chocolate Cake

Need a chocolate cake in a hurry? No mixer is required—just a bowl, a whisk, and a rubber spatula. This cake contains no eggs or dairy, making it very easy to make with ingredients at hand, while still producing a soft, moist, very chocolaty cake. It also happens to be vegan. Sift the cocoa before measuring to remove any lumps. As with any chocolate cake, this one pairs well with everything from Seven-Minute Frosting (page 45) to Italian Meringue Buttercream (page 42) in any of its variations or even Caramel Frosting (page 51).

Makes two 9 x 2-inch round layers

3 cups all-purpose flour

2 cups sugar

⅔ cup sifted natural cocoa

2 teaspoons baking soda

1 teaspoon salt

2 cups water, at room temperature

⅔ cup vegetable oil such as canola or safflower

2 tablespoons apple cider vinegar or distilled white vinegar

1 tablespoon vanilla extract

1. Position a rack in the middle of the oven. Preheat the oven to 350°F. Coat the insides of two 9 × 2-inch round cake pans with nonstick cooking spray, line the bottoms with parchment rounds, then spray the parchment.

2. Whisk together the flour, sugar, cocoa, baking soda, and salt in a large bowl.

3. Whisk together the water, oil, vinegar, and vanilla in a medium-size bowl.

4. Pour the wet ingredients over the dry ones and whisk until combined and smooth. Divide the batter evenly between the pans. Firmly tap the bottom of the pans on the work surface to dislodge any bubbles.

5. Bake for 30 to 35 minutes, or until a toothpick inserted into the layers shows a few moist crumbs when removed.

6. Cool the pans on wire racks for 8 to 10 minutes. Unmold, peel off the parchment, and place directly on the racks to cool completely. The layers are ready to fill and frost. Alternatively, place the cooled layers on cardboard rounds and double-wrap in plastic wrap; store at room temperature, and assemble or serve within 24 hours.

White Cake

Lighter in texture, paler in color, and subtler in flavor than yellow cake, white cake can be combined with delicate flavors such as Lemon Curd (page 54), Pastry Cream (page 53), and vanilla-, raspberry-, or liqueur-accented frostings. Feel free to experiment; when paired with Milk Chocolate Frosting (page 48) on a whim, the result was fabulous.

Makes two 9 x 2-inch round layers

3½ cups sifted cake flour

1 tablespoon plus 1 teaspoon baking powder

½ teaspoon salt

6 large egg whites, at room temperature

1½ cups whole milk, at room temperature

1 cup (2 sticks) unsalted butter, at room temperature, cut into small pieces

1½ cups sugar

2 teaspoons vanilla extract

1. Position a rack in the middle of the oven. Preheat the oven to 350°F. Coat the insides of two 9 × 2-inch round cake pans with nonstick cooking spray, line the bottoms with the parchment rounds, then spray the parchment.

2. Whisk together the flour, baking powder, and salt in a medium-size bowl to combine and aerate; set aside. Whisk together the egg whites and milk in a small bowl; set aside.

3. Beat the butter until creamy, about 2 minutes, with an electric mixer on medium-high speed. Add the sugar gradually and beat until very light and fluffy, about 3 minutes, scraping down the bowl once or twice. Beat in the vanilla.

4. Add the flour mixture in three additions, alternately with the egg white–milk mixture, while beating on low speed. Begin and end with the flour, and beat briefly until smooth. Divide the batter evenly between the pans and smooth the tops with an offset spatula.

5. Bake for 25 to 30 minutes, or until a toothpick inserted into the layers shows a few moist crumbs when removed. The layers will be light golden brown around the edges and top and will have come away from the sides of the pans.

6. Cool the pans on wire racks for 8 to 10 minutes. Unmold, peel off the parchment, and place the layers directly on the racks to cool completely. Once cool, the layers are ready to fill and frost. Alternatively, place the cooled layers on cardboard rounds and double-wrap in plastic wrap; store at room temperature, and assemble and serve within 24 hours.

Hot Milk Sponge Cake

This old-fashioned sponge cake is used in the Boston Cream Pie Birthday Cake (page 73) and the Tantalizing Fruit "Tart" Birthday Cake (page 142), or any time you want two simple vanilla sponge layers. Like all good birthday cakes, this recipe comes from a home cook—my most trusted baking friend Mary McNamara's mom, Eleanor. The batter will be thick, but will come together once the hot milk is added. When you beat the eggs and sugar, beat them until creamy, but do not overbeat or too much air will be incorporated and the cake might deflate upon baking. Once cooled, the cake can be sliced in half horizontally with a sharp knife into two layers.

Makes one 9 x 2-inch round cake

1 cup all-purpose flour

1 teaspoon baking powder

Generous ¼ teaspoon salt

½ cup whole milk

1½ tablespoons unsalted butter

2 large eggs, at room temperature

1 cup sugar

¾ teaspoon vanilla extract

1. Position a rack in the middle of the oven. Preheat the oven to 350°F. Coat the inside of a 9 × 2-inch round cake pan with nonstick cooking spray, line the bottom with a parchment round, and then spray the parchment.

2. Whisk together the flour, baking powder, and salt in a medium-size bowl to combine and aerate; set aside. Combine the milk and butter in a small saucepan and heat over medium heat until the butter is melted; set aside and cover to keep hot.

3. In a large bowl, using a large balloon whisk, beat the eggs until combined and frothy, about 10 seconds. Add the sugar and whisk until very creamy and light in color, 1 to 2 minutes; beat in the vanilla.

4. Add the flour mixture all at once and whisk it in; the batter will be thick. Add the hot milk mixture all at once and whisk it in until the ingredients are combined and the batter is smooth. Scrape the batter into the prepared pan.

5. Bake for 20 to 25 minutes, or until a toothpick inserted into the cake shows a few moist crumbs when removed. The cake should be light golden brown on top and spring back when pressed gently on top.

6. Cool the pan on a wire rack for 8 to 10 minutes. Unmold, peel off the parchment, and place the layer directly on the rack to cool completely. The cake is ready to be sliced in half horizontally, filled, and frosted. Alternatively, place the cooled cake on a cardboard round and double-wrap in plastic wrap; store at room temperature, and assemble and serve within 24 hours.

Angel Food Cake

Dry ingredients gently folded into whipped egg whites give angel food cakes their name and lightness. An added plus is that this cake, unembellished, is considered fat-free per serving. You will need an angel food cake pan, available at any housewares store. Once baked, the cake is inverted (while still in its pan) to allow it to cool: It's so light, it might fall in on itself if cooled upright.

Makes one 10-inch cake

1 cup sifted cake flour
¾ cup sifted confectioners' sugar
Pinch of salt
12 large egg whites, at room temperature
1½ teaspoons cream of tartar
⅔ cup superfine sugar
1½ teaspoons vanilla extract
¼ teaspoon almond extract (optional)

Baker's Tip The optional almond extract adds a slight background flavor that balances out the inherent sweetness. Angel food cake pairs nicely with whipped cream, fresh or stewed fruit, Lemon Curd (page 54), or even a scoop of ice cream or sorbet on the side.

1. Position a rack in the lower third of the oven. Preheat the oven to 350°F. You will need a 10-inch, two-piece (loose-bottom) tube pan; leave it ungreased.

2. Whisk together the flour, confectioners' sugar, and salt in a medium-size bowl to combine and aerate; set aside.

3. Beat the egg whites until frothy with an electric mixer on medium-high speed. Add the cream of tartar and continue to beat until soft peaks form. Add the superfine sugar gradually and continue beating until stiff, shiny peaks form. Beat in the vanilla and almond extracts.

4. Sprinkle about one-third of the dry ingredients over the egg whites. Using an up-and-over folding action with a large balloon whisk, gently incorporate the dry ingredients into egg whites, taking care not to deflate them. Add another third of the dry mixture and continue folding with whisk. Fold in the remaining dry ingredients using a large rubber spatula. Carefully spoon the batter into the ungreased pan, smoothing the top with a small offset spatula.

5. Bake for 30 to 35 minutes, or until a wooden skewer inserted into the cake comes out clean.

6. Remove the cake from the oven and immediately prop the cake pan upside down on the neck of a narrow bottle to cool completely. Once the cake has cooled, run an icing spatula around the sides of the cake. Apply pressure out toward the pan or you might accidentally shave off some of the cake's sides. Turn over to unmold and place on a serving platter. The flat bottom of the cake is now the top. The cake is ready to serve. Alternatively, unmold the cooled cake directly onto a cardboard round and double-wrap in plastic wrap; store at room temperature, and assemble and serve within 24 hours.

Spice Cake

Cinnamon, cloves, nutmeg, ginger, and cardamom are used with a light hand so the spices don't overpower the cake. The buttermilk yields a crumb that is soft and tender. If you have a choice between nonfat and low-fat buttermilk, use the low-fat. This cake is fabulous with Seven-Minute Frosting (page 45), Cream Cheese Frosting (page 52), or Caramel Frosting (page 51).

Makes two 9 x 2-inch round layers

3 cups sifted cake flour

1 generous teaspoon baking soda

¼ teaspoon salt

¾ cup (1½ sticks) unsalted butter, at room temperature, cut into tablespoon-sized pieces

¾ cup sugar

1½ teaspoons ground cinnamon

¾ teaspoon freshly grated nutmeg

¼ teaspoon ground cardamom

¼ teaspoon ground cloves

¼ teaspoon ground ginger

2 large eggs, at room temperature

1 cup plus 2 tablespoons buttermilk, at room temperature

1. Position a rack in the middle of the oven. Preheat the oven to 350°F. Coat the insides of two 9 × 2-inch round cake pans with nonstick cooking spray, line the bottoms with parchment rounds, then spray the parchment.

2. Whisk together the flour, baking soda, and salt in a medium-size bowl to combine and aerate; set aside.

3. Beat the butter until creamy, about 2 minutes with an electric mixer on medium-high speed. Add the sugar gradually and beat until very light and fluffy, about 3 minutes, scraping down the bowl once or twice. Beat in the cinnamon, nutmeg, cardamom, cloves, and ginger.

4. Beat in the eggs one at a time, scraping down after each addition and allowing each egg to be absorbed before continuing. Add the flour mixture in three additions, alternately with the buttermilk, while beating on low speed. Begin and end with the flour and beat briefly until smooth. Divide the batter evenly between the pans and smooth the tops with an offset spatula.

5. Bake for 20 to 25 minutes, or until a toothpick inserted into the layers shows a few moist crumbs when removed. The layers will be tinged with light golden brown around the edges and top and will have begun to come away from the sides of the pans.

6. Cool the pans on wire racks for 8 to 10 minutes. Unmold, peel off the parchment, and place the layers directly on the racks to cool completely. The layers are ready to fill and frost. Alternatively, place the cooled layers on cardboard rounds and double-wrap in plastic wrap; store at room temperature, and assemble and serve within 24 hours.

Carrot Cake

This moist carrot cake features raisins, nuts, and orange—the raisins are plumped in orange juice. The three tall layers make an impressive cake that will serve a large crowd. As an alternative to the classic pairing of Cream Cheese Frosting (page 52), try the white chocolate variation of Italian Meringue Buttercream (page 42).

Makes three 9 x 2-inch round layers

¼ cup orange juice

1¼ cups dark raisins

2 cups all-purpose flour

2 teaspoons baking powder

1 teaspoon baking soda

1 teaspoon salt

1¼ cups vegetable oil such as canola or safflower

2 cups lightly packed light brown sugar

4 large eggs, at room temperature

2 teaspoons ground cinnamon

2 teaspoons vanilla extract

4 cups lightly packed, finely grated carrots (about 1 pound)

1¼ cups toasted walnut or pecan halves, chopped

1. Position the racks in the upper and lower thirds of the oven (you'll use both racks). Preheat the oven to 350°F. Coat the insides of three 9 × 2-inch round cake pans with nonstick cooking spray, line the bottoms with parchment rounds, then spray the parchment.

2. Combine the orange juice and raisins in a small saucepan and bring to a boil over high heat; remove from the heat and steep for 10 minutes. You can also heat the juice in the microwave; just bring it to a boil, and allow the same steeping time.

3. Whisk together the flour, baking powder, baking soda, and salt in a large bowl to combine and aerate; set aside.

4. Whisk together the oil and brown sugar until well blended in a medium-size bowl. Whisk in the eggs one at a time, until each one is absorbed. Whisk in the cinnamon and vanilla, then stir in the carrots, nuts, and raisins with any liquid.

5. Pour the wet ingredients over the dry ones and whisk until combined. Divide the batter between the pans and smooth the tops with an offset spatula.

6. Bake for 25 to 35 minutes, or until a toothpick inserted into the layers shows a few moist crumbs when removed.

7. Cool the pans on wire racks for 10 to 12 minutes. Unmold, peel off the parchment, and place the layers directly on the racks to cool completely. The layers are ready to fill and frost. Alternatively, place the cooled layers on cardboard rounds and double-wrap in plastic wrap; store at room temperature, and assemble and serve within 24 hours.

Banana Cake

This is a very flavorful, rich, moist banana cake that lends itself to variations: Add chocolate chips, walnuts, or raisins or other dried fruit for a new take on this classic. Make sure to use very ripe bananas—they should show absolutely no green and have some black spots. Do not puree the bananas; rather, slice them into a bowl and mash with a potato masher. This makes a large three-layered cake.

Makes three 9 x 2-inch round layers

3 cups all-purpose flour

2 teaspoons baking powder

1 teaspoon baking soda

½ teaspoon salt

1 cup toasted pecan halves, chopped

¾ cup (1½ sticks) unsalted butter, at room temperature, cut into pieces

2 cups sugar

1½ teaspoons vanilla extract

3 large eggs, at room temperature

2½ cups coarsely mashed bananas (about 5 large bananas)

½ cup sour cream, yogurt, or buttermilk, at room temperature

1. Position the racks in the upper and lower thirds of the oven (you'll use both racks). Preheat the oven to 350°F. Coat the insides of three 9 × 2-inch round cake pans with nonstick cooking spray, line the bottoms with parchment rounds, then spray the parchment.

2. Whisk together flour, baking powder, baking soda, and salt in a medium-size bowl to combine and aerate; toss in nuts and set aside.

3. In a large bowl, with an electric mixer on medium-high speed, beat the butter until creamy, about 2 minutes. Add the sugar gradually and beat until very light and fluffy, about 3 minutes, scraping down the bowl once or twice. Beat in the vanilla.

4. Beat in the eggs one at a time, scraping down after each addition and allowing each egg to be absorbed before continuing. Beat in the bananas. Add the flour mixture in three additions, alternately with the sour cream, while beating on low speed. Begin and end with the flour and beat briefly until smooth. Divide the batter evenly among the pans and smooth the tops with an offset spatula.

5. Bake for 40 to 50 minutes, or until a toothpick inserted into the layers shows a few moist crumbs when removed. The layers will be a light golden brown.

6. Cool the pans on wire racks for 10 to 12 minutes. Unmold, peel off the parchment, and place the layers directly on the racks to cool completely. The layers are ready to fill and frost. Alternatively, place the cooled layers on cardboard rounds and double-wrap in plastic wrap; store at room temperature, and assemble and serve within 24 hours.

Basic Frostings, Buttercreams, and Fillings

Turn to this chapter for all of your frosting and filling needs. You will find all the basics such as Confectioners' Sugar Frosting and Italian Meringue Buttercream, as well as Cream Cheese Frosting, Chocolate Ganache Glaze and Frosting, Lemon Curd, Candy Plastic, and more. These are used as components of the cakes in the Birthday Cakes chapter, but they are also meant to be a resource when inventing your own creative cakes.

Confectioners' Sugar Frosting

This easy frosting is the go-to version for many cake bakers. Most frostings that use confectioners' sugar have a bit of leeway. If the frosting is too thin, add a bit more confectioners' sugar; if too thick, thin with a little milk. The key to making this silky smooth and creamy is to beat it longer than you might think necessary; once it is smooth, keep beating for a couple of minutes more.

Makes 3¾ cups

¾ cup (1½ sticks) unsalted butter, at room temperature, cut into small pieces

6¾ cups confectioners' sugar (plus extra as needed), whisked before measuring

⅓ cup whole milk (plus extra as needed)

1½ teaspoons vanilla extract

1. In a large bowl, with an electric mixer on medium-high speed, beat the butter until creamy, about 2 minutes. Add 1 cup of the sugar gradually, beating until light and fluffy, about 3 minutes, scraping down the bowl once or twice. Add the remaining sugar, milk, and vanilla and beat on high speed until silky smooth.

2. The frosting is now ready to use. It is best if used immediately; it may be refrigerated in an airtight container for 4 days. (Bring it to room temperature and rebeat after storing.)

Fluffy Meringue Frosting

If you have been looking for a fat-free vanilla frosting, this is it! It is bright white, very sweet, and has a marshmallow quality to it in terms of texture and taste. You might notice that the recipe is the same as the Italian Meringue Buttercream—but without the butter. Make sure that no grease (from your hands or utensils) comes in contact with the frosting, or the meringue will deflate. It must be used right away.

Makes 4½ cups

½ cup plus 2 tablespoons sugar

3 tablespoons water

3 large egg whites, at room temperature

½ teaspoon cream of tartar

½ teaspoon vanilla extract

1. Place ½ cup of the sugar and the water in a small saucepan. Stir to wet the sugar. Bring to a boil over medium-high heat, swirling the pan occasionally. Dip a pastry brush in cold water and wash down the sugar crystals from the sides of the pan once or twice. Turn down the heat to simmer gently.

2. Meanwhile, place the egg whites in a clean, grease-free stand mixer bowl and whip until frothy on low speed using the balloon whip attachment. Add the cream of tartar and turn the speed up to medium-high. When soft peaks form, add the remaining 2 tablespoons sugar gradually. Continue whipping until stiff, glossy peaks form.

3. Bring the sugar-water mixture to a rapid boil and cook until it reaches 248° to 250°F. As the syrup cooks, check for visual clues to assess temperature: It starts out thin with many small bubbles over the entire surface. As the water evaporates, the mixture will become visibly thicker. The bubbles become larger and pop open more slowly. At this point, the syrup definitely looks thickened, but it has not begun to color; this is the firm ball stage. If you drop a bit of the syrup into a glass of cold water, it will form into a ball. When you squeeze the ball between your fingertips, it will feel firm.

4. When the syrup is ready, pour a thin, steady stream over the meringue, without pouring any on the rotating whip or the sides of the bowl. Whip the meringue until cool to the touch. Beat in the vanilla. The frosting is now ready to use and best if used immediately.

Italian Meringue Buttercream

This is an ultra-smooth, not-too-sweet buttercream and my frosting of choice, not only because of its exceptional texture and flavor, but because it can be endlessly varied. You can add chocolate, liqueurs, pureed fruits, juices, or even coffee. A stand mixer is best for this recipe, as it has to be beaten for quite a while; a candy thermometer is also helpful. It is crucial that any cake frosted with this buttercream be served at room temperature, or the texture and flavor will suffer.

The standard recipe below makes enough to fill and frost a three- or four-layer cake with lots of swirls and decorations on the outside. The large batch is the maximum amount that can be made in a 5-quart stand mixer.

Standard batch; makes about 6 cups

1¼ cups sugar

⅓ cup water

6 large egg whites, at room temperature

¾ teaspoon cream of tartar

2¼ cups (4½ sticks) unsalted butter, at room temperature, cut into pieces

Large batch; makes about 7½ cups

1¼ cups plus ⅓ cup sugar

½ cup water

8 large egg whites, at room temperature

1 teaspoon cream of tartar

1½ pounds (6 sticks) unsalted butter, at room temperature, cut into pieces

1. Place 1 cup of the sugar (if making a standard batch) or 1¼ cups of the sugar (if making a large batch) and the water in a small saucepan. Stir to wet the sugar. Bring to a boil over medium-high heat, swirling the pan occasionally. Dip a pastry brush in cold water and wash down the sugar crystals from the sides of the pan once or twice. Allow the sugar mixture to simmer gently as you proceed with the egg whites.

2. Meanwhile, place the egg whites in a clean, grease-free stand mixer bowl and whip until frothy on low speed using the balloon whip attachment. Add the cream of tartar and turn the speed up to medium-high. When soft peaks form, gradually add the remaining sugar. Continue whipping until stiff, glossy peaks form.

3. Bring the sugar-water mixture to a rapid boil and cook until it reaches 248° to 250°F. As the syrup cooks, check for visual clues to assess temperature: It starts out thin with many small bubbles over the entire surface. As the water evaporates, the mixture will become visibly thicker. The bubbles become larger and pop open more slowly. At this point, the syrup definitely looks thickened, but it has not begun to color; this is the firm ball stage. If you drop a bit of the syrup into a glass of cold water, it will form into a ball. When you squeeze the ball between your fingertips, it will feel firm.

4. When the syrup is ready, pour a thin, steady stream directly over the meringue. Do not pour any onto the whisk or the sides of the bowl. Whip the meringue until cool to the touch; this step is very important. With the machine running, add the butter a couple of tablespoons at a time. Keep beating until the buttercream is completely smooth.

5. The buttercream is now ready to use. (Any flavorings may be added at this point; variations are given on page 44.) It may be refrigerated for up to 1 week in an airtight container or frozen for up to 1 month. If frozen, defrost in the refrigerator overnight and bring to warm room temperature before rebeating. Always rebeat before using.

NOTE: *This buttercream freezes very well, so I make as much as possible at one time, use what I need, and keep any extra on hand in the freezer. If you have a 5-quart stand mixer and want to make the most you can at once, make a large batch. You'll need to make two large batches for The Big Birthday Cake, page 67.*

Baker's Tip

Temperature is key with this buttercream. If the meringue is warm when the butter is added, it will melt the butter and become soupy. If the butter is too cold, the buttercream will be lumpy and too firm. If your buttercream is too soft and loose, simply chill it over an ice bath. Chill for several minutes before proceeding. If the mixture is too stiff, just keep whipping; it might smooth out. You can also aim a hot hair dryer at the outside of the bowl; it will warm up the buttercream quickly. Or place a cup of too-firm buttercream in the microwave for a few seconds, then add it back to the larger amount to smooth out the overall texture.

Italian Meringue Buttercream Variations

See pages 42–43 for master recipe.

Vanilla Buttercream

Add 1 tablespoon vanilla extract to the standard batch; add 1⅓ tablespoons to the large batch.

Liqueur-Flavored Buttercream

Add approximately ⅓ cup of liqueur to the standard batch; add a scant ½ cup to the large batch. Adjust the taste as needed. Some liqueurs will require less, some more. The texture of the buttercream will guide you also; you do not want it to get too loose. Try Grand Marnier, Cointreau, amaretto, Kahlúa, or rum, to name a few.

White, Milk, or Dark Chocolate Buttercream

Note that white chocolate will make the buttercream a creamy ivory color, milk chocolate buttercream will have an almost pinkish tinge, and semi- or bittersweet chocolate buttercream will be a milk chocolate color. Add 12 ounces of melted and cooled white, milk, semisweet, or bittersweet chocolate to the standard batch; add 1 pound to the large batch. Whip until the chocolate is thoroughly incorporated.

Espresso Buttercream

The bitterness of coffee tempers the sweetness of the buttercream. Dissolve 2 tablespoons instant espresso powder (such as Medaglia d'Oro) in 2 tablespoons boiling water or warmed Kahlúa and add to the standard batch; add 2 tablespoons plus 2 teaspoons of each to the large batch. Whip well to incorporate. The coffee flavor can be adjusted according to your preference.

Raspberry Buttercream

This buttercream is a fabulous bright pink color. Individually quick-frozen berries (without sugar) work perfectly. Defrost and puree berries in food processor. I leave the seeds in, but they may be strained out, if you wish. Slowly add purée to the buttercream. It may appear soupy, but with continued beating, it will absorb the puree. You can adjust the amount of puree to your taste, making it as strong in color and flavor as desired, but at some point, the buttercream will not absorb any more. A standard batch can take up to about 1 cup of puree; a large batch should absorb up to 1⅓ cups.

Lemon Curd Buttercream

Add 1 cup lemon curd to the standard batch; add 1⅓ cups to the large batch. Beat well to incorporate.

Seven-Minute Frosting

This is a classic white, marshmallow-like fluffy frosting that also happens to be fat free. Two rules for success: The egg whites must be beaten without interruption over heat until they reach 160°F, and then they must be beaten off the heat until the frosting is cool to the touch. This may very well take longer than seven minutes; the timing is not important. What is important is that you whip the frosting until it is completely cooled and stiff peaks have formed. You need a hand-held mixer and a candy thermometer for this recipe. It is sweeter, develops more of a crust, and does not hold up quite as well as the Fluffy Meringue Frosting on page 41.

Makes 3½ cups

3 large egg whites, at room temperature
1½ cups sugar
3 tablespoons water
1 tablespoon light corn syrup
½ teaspoon cream of tartar
Pinch of salt
1 teaspoon vanilla extract

1. Place the egg whites, sugar, water, corn syrup, cream of tartar, and salt in the top of a double boiler and whisk to combine.

2. Place the top of the double boiler over the bottom filled with simmering water and clip a candy thermometer on the side of pan so that it is submerged in the mixture. Make sure the top of your double boiler touches the simmering water in the bottom pot. Immediately begin beating with hand-held mixer on medium speed and beat for 1 minute. Increase the speed to high.

3. Keep whipping the mixture until the temperature reaches 160°F. Remove the top of the double boiler and continue whipping the frosting until it is cool to the touch and stiff peaks have formed, about 7 minutes more; just keep beating until it is thick enough. Once the desired texture is achieved, beat in the vanilla. The frosting is now ready to use and best if used immediately.

Rich Egg Yolk Buttercream

This very rich buttercream is best used for fillings in cakes for adults; their palates will appreciate it most. It can be flavored similarly to Italian Meringue Buttercream; use those variations as a guide, remembering that this recipe is half the yield of the standard batch. As with the Italian Meringue Buttercream, this freezes well and is best made in a stand mixer.

Makes about 3 cups

¾ cup sugar

⅓ cup water

6 large egg yolks, at room temperature

1¼ cups (2½ sticks) unsalted butter, at room temperature, cut into pieces

1. Place the sugar and water in a small saucepan. Stir to wet the sugar. Bring to a boil over medium-high heat, swirling the pan occasionally. Dip a pastry brush in cold water and wash down the sugar crystals from the sides of the pan once or twice. Allow the sugar mixture to simmer gently as you proceed with the egg yolks.

2. Meanwhile, place the egg yolks in a stand mixer bowl and whip on high speed using the balloon whip attachment until thick, creamy, and light in color.

3. Bring the sugar-water mixture to a rapid boil and cook until it reaches 248° to 250°F. As the syrup cooks, check for visual clues to assess temperature: It starts out thin with many small bubbles over the entire surface. As the water evaporates, the mixture will become visibly thicker. The bubbles become larger and pop open more slowly. At this point, the syrup definitely looks thickened, but it has not begun to color; this is the firm ball stage. If you drop a bit of the syrup into a glass of cold water, it will form into a ball. When you squeeze the ball between your fingertips, it will feel firm.

4. When the syrup is ready, pour a thin, steady stream directly over the yolks. Do not pour any onto the whisk or the sides of the bowl. Whip until cool to the touch; this step is very important. With the machine running, add the butter a couple of tablespoons at a time. Keep beating until the buttercream is completely smooth.

5. The buttercream is now ready to use. (Any flavorings may be added at this point.) It may be refrigerated in an airtight container for 1 week or frozen for up to 1 month. If frozen, defrost in the refrigerator overnight and bring to warm room temperature before rebeating. Always rebeat before using.

Fudgy Chocolate Frosting

Chocolaty, rich, and creamy, this frosting is not based on actual fudge, but it is loaded with chocolaty, fudgy flavor. For a lighter chocolate frosting, use the chocolate variation of the Italian Meringue Buttercream (page 42); for even darker, richer chocolate frosting, use the Chocolate Ganache Glaze and Frosting (page 49). Like all confectioners' sugar–based frostings, the texture can be adjusted by adding more confectioners' sugar to thicken it or more milk to thin it out.

Makes about 3½ cups

½ cup (1 stick) unsalted butter, at room temperature, cut into pieces

4 cups confectioners' sugar (plus extra as needed), whisked before measuring

5 ounces unsweetened chocolate, melted and slightly cooled

1½ teaspoons vanilla extract

⅓ cup whole milk (plus extra as needed)

⅓ cup heavy cream (plus extra as needed)

1. In a large bowl, with an electric mixer on medium-high speed, beat the butter until creamy, about 2 minutes. Add 1 cup of the sugar gradually, beating until it begins to combine, about 2 minutes, scraping down the bowl once or twice. Add the remaining sugar, the melted chocolate, vanilla, milk, and cream, and beat on high speed until completely smooth and creamy.

2. The frosting is now ready to use. It is best if used immediately; it may be refrigerated in an airtight container for up to 4 days. (Bring it to room temperature and rebeat after storing.)

Milk Chocolate Frosting

This creamy chocolate frosting is great with white cake, chocolate cake, and banana cake—anywhere a milk chocolate flavor would be complementary. It is quick and easy to make, too.

Makes 3½ cups

1 cup heavy cream

9 ounces milk chocolate, finely chopped

½ cup (1 stick) unsalted butter, at room temperature, cut into pieces

2 cups confectioners' sugar (plus extra as needed), whisked before measuring

½ teaspoon vanilla extract

1. Melt the cream and chocolate together in a microwave or in the top of a double boiler set over simmering water. Cool at room temperature, stirring occasionally to release the heat, until it is as thick as mayonnaise. (You may hasten cooling over an ice bath.)

2. In a large bowl, with an electric mixer on medium-high speed, beat the butter until creamy, about 2 minutes. Add 1 cup of the sugar gradually, beating until light and fluffy, about 3 minutes, scraping down the bowl once or twice. Add the remaining sugar, the chocolate mixture, and vanilla, and beat on high speed until silky smooth.

3. The frosting is now ready to use. It is best if used immediately; it may be refrigerated in an airtight container for up to 4 days. (Bring it to room temperature and rebeat after storing.)

Chocolate Ganache Glaze and Frosting

Ganache is the darkest, richest chocolate icing in this book. You can use it in its fluid state as a glaze, which will set if a cake is refrigerated, or allow it to firm up at room temperature until it is spreadable or pipeable. The chocolate you use will greatly affect the result in terms of flavor, texture, and fluidity; I prefer Valrhona Equatoriale Dark, Merckens Yucatan, or Ghirardelli Semisweet. Consider this recipe a general guideline and feel free to make the frosting thicker or thinner as desired. When using darker, higher-cacao-percentage chocolates, the ganache will often "break" and not come together. Whisk in some extra cold cream and/or buzz it with an immersion blender (if you have one), and it will come back together.

Makes about 2½ cups

1¼ cups heavy cream
12 ounces semisweet or bittersweet chocolate, finely chopped

1. Place the cream in a large saucepan and bring to a boil over medium heat.

2. Remove from the heat and immediately sprinkle the chocolate into the cream. Cover and allow to sit for 5 minutes. The heat of the cream should melt the chocolate. Gently stir the ganache until smooth. If the chocolate is not melting, place the pan over very low heat, stirring often, until the chocolate is melted (take care not to burn the mixture).

3. The ganache is ready to use. Pour it over cakes as a glaze, or let the ganache firm up at room temperature overnight, until it is a spreadable consistency between mayonnaise and peanut butter. At this point you may apply it with an icing spatula or place it in a pastry bag with a decorating tip of choice. (You may hasten the chilling process by stirring the ganache over an ice bath. If it becomes too firm, or if you would like to return it to a liquid state, place it over hot water or microwave briefly.) Chocolate Ganache Glaze and Frosting may be refrigerated for up to 1 week in an airtight container or frozen for up to 1 month.

Sour Cream Chocolate Frosting

I can eat this frosting by the spoonful—it is so rich, chocolaty, and decadent. Different chocolates will affect the thickness of the final frosting; I prefer Valrhona Equatoriale Dark, Merckens Yucatan, or Ghirardelli Semisweet. If desired, add a little extra sour cream to thin out the frosting.

Makes about 3 cups

14 ounces semisweet chocolate, melted and warm (not hot)

1½ cups sour cream (plus extra as needed), at room temperature

Have the warm melted chocolate in a large bowl. Fold in the sour cream just until no white streaks remain. The frosting will become too thick with too much folding but remain silky if not overworked. If it becomes too stiff, you can warm it gently over a pot of warm water. The frosting is now ready to use and is best if used immediately.

Caramel Frosting

If you like caramel, butterscotch, and toffee flavors, you will find this frosting irresistible. It comes together very quickly but it must also be applied to your cake right away, as it sets up fast! Have your cake layers ready to go before starting this recipe. It is creamy for a brief few minutes, after which it becomes very firm and a bit sugary. You can substitute light brown sugar, but I think the dark brown accentuates the fabulous, deep caramel flavor. Try it with the Spice Cake or any of the chocolate cakes.

Makes about 3 cups

1½ cups lightly packed dark brown sugar

¾ cup (1½ sticks) unsalted butter, at room temperature, cut into pieces

½ cup plus 1 tablespoon heavy cream

3 cups confectioners' sugar (plus extra as needed), whisked before measuring

2 teaspoons vanilla extract

1. Combine the brown sugar, butter, and cream in a medium-size saucepan and bring to a simmer over medium-high heat. Simmer for 2 minutes, stirring frequently.

2. Remove from the heat and whisk in the confectioners' sugar and vanilla until smooth and spreadable. This will happen very quickly. Use the frosting immediately. Quickly fill your cake. For the top and sides of the cake, quickly pour the remaining frosting on top of the cake all at once, then quickly spread it around and down over the sides with an icing spatula. If it sets up too quickly, dip your icing spatula in hot water.

Cream Cheese Frosting

Here is a classic cream cheese frosting for carrot cakes and many other cakes as well. It is very creamy, spreads like a dream, and is not too sweet—but sweet enough.

Makes 3⅔ cups

1 pound full-fat or Neufchâtel cream cheese, at room temperature, cut into pieces

6 tablespoons (¾ stick) unsalted butter, at room temperature, cut into pieces

2⅔ cups confectioners' sugar, whisked before measuring

1. In a large bowl, with an electric mixer on medium-high speed, beat the cream cheese until smooth, about 2 minutes; you want to eliminate any lumps. Add the butter and beat on medium-high speed until very smooth, scraping down the bowl once or twice. Add half the sugar, beating on low speed until absorbed, then add the remaining sugar and beat until smooth and creamy.

2. The frosting is now ready to use. It is best if used immediately, but may be refrigerated in an airtight container for up to 4 days. (Bring it to room temperature and rebeat after storing.)

Whipped Cream Frosting

For this simple frosting, lightly sweetened cream is whipped so that soft, but firm, peaks form. To make decorations, whip the frosting a bit more to hold its shape. The cornstarch in confectioners' sugar helps stabilize the finished whipped cream.

Makes about 4 cups

2½ cups heavy cream

5 tablespoons confectioners' sugar, whisked before measuring

½ teaspoon vanilla extract

1. In a chilled large bowl, with an electric mixer on medium-high speed, whip the cream until it just begins to thicken. Add the confectioners' sugar and vanilla and beat until soft, but firm, peaks form. If using as a frosting, it is ready at this point.

2. If you want to pipe designs, whip until stiffer peaks form, but do not overbeat. If it shows clumps and lumps, it is overwhipped. Simply stir in some liquid cream to smooth it out. The frosting should be used immediately.

Pastry Cream

If you look at various recipes for pastry cream you will see subtle differences in the amounts and types of ingredients (egg yolks, whole eggs, or both; flour or cornstarch; and so on). This is a very straightforward version with a nice vanilla flavor. It is rather thick, as it is meant to slice well when spread between cake layers; I would not use this version in éclairs or classic fruit tarts where a softer pastry cream is preferred. If there are lumps in the pastry cream when you remove it from the heat, don't panic. Pour it through a fine-mesh strainer, then discard the solids in the strainer; pastry chefs do it all the time.

Makes about 1⅔ cups

1¼ cup whole milk
¼ cup sugar
3 large egg yolks, at room temperature
2½ tablespoons all-purpose flour
2 tablespoons cornstarch
Pinch of salt
1½ teaspoons vanilla extract

1. Place the milk in a medium-size nonreactive saucepan. Bring to a boil over medium heat; remove from the heat and keep warm.

2. Meanwhile, whisk together the sugar and yolks in a medium-size bowl until creamy. Whisk in the flour, cornstarch, and salt until smooth.

3. Pour about one-quarter of the warm milk over the egg yolk mixture, whisking gently. Add the remaining milk and whisk to combine. Immediately pour the mixture back into the pan and cook over low-medium heat. Whisk almost continuously and watch for bubbles. As soon as the mixture begins to boil, whisk vigorously and cook for 1 to 2 minutes to keep the pastry cream from scorching. The pastry cream should be thick enough to mound when dropped from a spoon. Remove from the heat and whisk in the vanilla.

4. Allow the pastry cream to cool; stir occasionally to release heat. When almost at room temperature, scrape into an airtight container, press some plastic wrap on the surface to keep a skin from forming, snap on the cover, and refrigerate for at least 4 hours, or until thoroughly chilled. Pastry Cream can be refrigerated for up to 3 days.

Lemon Curd

This tart, smooth lemon filling is easy to put together and makes a puckery addition to cakes where lemon flavor is desired. Use it as a filling, not as a frosting, although it can be folded into Italian Meringue Buttercream for a lemony frosting. The zest adds more flavor, but if you prefer a smooth texture, omit it.

Makes 1½ cups

¼ cup freshly squeezed lemon juice

2 large eggs plus 1 large egg yolk, at room temperature

¾ cup sugar

6 tablespoons (¾ stick) unsalted butter, at room temperature, cut into pieces

½ teaspoon finely grated lemon zest (optional)

1. Place the juice, eggs, yolks, and sugar in the top of a double boiler. Whisk together to break up the eggs. Add the butter. Place the top pot over the bottom pot of the double boiler filled with simmering water that just touches the bottom of the top pot.

2. Whisk the mixture frequently over simmering water for about 12 minutes, or until the mixture reaches 180°F. (Reaching the right temperature is most important, and the curd itself should not simmer.) The curd will thicken and form a soft shape when a spoon is stirred through. If desired, stir in the zest after removing from heat. Let cool to room temperature, scrape into an airtight container, and refrigerate overnight or up to 1 week.

Candy Plastic

By combining melted chocolate-like candies and corn syrup, you can create a malleable candy clay perfect for making roses, leaves, and ribbons (see pages 20 and 149 for instructions). I use Wilton Candy Melts, which come in a rainbow of colors and cocoa and vanilla flavors; you may use whichever ones you like.

Makes about 2 pounds

28 ounces Wilton Candy Melts, finely chopped

⅔ cup light corn syrup

1. Melt the candy in the top of a double boiler or microwave. Stir in the corn syrup until the mixture comes together. It might look grainy, which is okay; it will smooth out when kneaded. Scrape onto a large piece of plastic wrap and wrap well.

2. Let sit until firm enough to roll out—at least 6 hours, or preferably overnight, at cool room temperature.

3. The candy plastic is ready to use. It may be stored for 2 weeks at room temperature. Keep tightly wrapped.

The Birthday Cakes

This chapter is arranged alphabetically. To find cakes with specific

flavors, ingredients, or uses, see the handy lists starting on page 157,

where you'll find them grouped by such categories as Easy Cakes,

Elegant and Sophisticated Cakes, Cakes for the Kid in Everyone, and more.

Amaretto-Chocolate Cheesecake

Chocolate and cheesecake combined with the distinctive flavor of amaretto make for an impressive, elegant birthday cake. This one is dark and rich, with plenty of melted chocolate and a touch of amaretto in the batter along with amaretti cookies in the crust. I use Lazzaroni Amaretti di Saronno cookies, which are available in Italian food shops and can be ordered online, and Disaronno amaretto liqueur. The whipped cream and chocolate shavings on the top give the cake a celebratory look—and believe it or not, the whipped cream lightens the cake, so don't leave it out.

**Makes one 9-inch round cake;
serves 14 to 16**

Crust

One 9-ounce box Nabisco Famous Chocolate Wafers, finely ground

8 individual Lazzaroni Amaretti di Saronno cookies, finely ground

7 tablespoons (¾ stick plus 1 tablespoon) unsalted butter, melted

Filling

1½ pounds full-fat cream cheese, at room temperature, cut into pieces

1 cup sugar

3 large eggs, at room temperature

10 ounces semisweet chocolate, melted

3 tablespoons amaretto

1 cup full-fat sour cream

Frosting

1 cup heavy cream

2 tablespoons confectioners' sugar

1 tablespoon amaretto

One 1-ounce block semisweet chocolate

Pastry bag

Large star decorating tip such as Wilton #2110 or Ateco #835

Baker's Tip

No water bath is necessary here, because the large amount of chocolate in this cheesecake stabilizes the batter so the cake doesn't crack. Both types of cookies are best ground in the food processor fitted with the metal blade.

1. Position a rack in the middle of the oven. Preheat the oven to 350°F. Coat the inside of a 9 × 3-inch round loose-bottom or springform pan with nonstick cooking spray.

2. For the crust: Place both kinds of cookie crumbs and the melted butter in a bowl and stir to combine. Press the crust evenly over the bottom and up about 1½ inches on the sides of the prepared pan. Bake the crust for about 12 minutes, or until just dry to the touch. Place the pan on a wire rack to cool while preparing the filling.

3. For the cheesecake: Beat the cream cheese until creamy, about 3 minutes, in a large bowl with an electric mixer on medium-high. Add the sugar gradually and beat until very light and fluffy, about 3 minutes, scraping down the bowl once or twice. Beat in the eggs one at a time, scraping down after each addition and allowing each egg to be absorbed before continuing. Beat in the chocolate and liqueur. Stir in the sour cream by hand until completely incorporated. Pour the batter over the crust.

4. Bake for 55 minutes to 1 hour. The top will look dry and smooth, but the cake will still jiggle when you gently shake the pan. Turn off the oven and let the cake sit in the oven for 1 more hour. Cover and refrigerate the cake overnight, or up to 2 days, before proceeding. (The cake may be double-wrapped in plastic wrap at this point, still in the pan to protect it, and frozen for up to 1 month.)

5. For the frosting: Whip the cream in a chilled large bowl with an electric mixer on medium-high speed until it begins to thicken. Add the confectioners' sugar and liqueur and beat until stiff peaks form. The frosting is ready to use.

6. Unmolding the cheesecake: Warm an icing spatula under hot running water and shake dry. Run the spatula around the sides of the cake to release it from the pan. Apply pressure out toward the pan, not in toward the cake, or you might accidentally shave off some of the cake's sides. If using a loose-bottom pan, press the bottom up to release. If using a springform, unlock and remove the pan sides. The cheesecake will still be on the round metal bottom of the pan. Affix this pan to a cardboard round of the same size with some frosting. (If you are brave, you can slide an icing spatula under the cheesecake crust, remove the metal bottom, and place the cake directly on the cardboard.) Place the frosting in a pastry bag fitted with a large star tip and pipe decorative shapes over the entire top of the cake. Grate the chocolate on the large holes of a box grater and scatter over the frosting. Refrigerate for at least 1 hour to allow the frosting to set.

7. Slice the cheesecake with a thin-bladed knife (dip the knife in hot water between cuts). Serve the cake cold.

Angel Food Cake with Berries

Birthday cakes can be light, luscious, and low-fat, yet still quite festive. If the birthday girl or boy has to watch fat intake, this is a perfect celebration dessert. The angel food cake alone is sweet and light. The deep red juices from the berries seep into the cake and create an interior that looks like red, pink, and white marble, while adding flavor and moistness.

Makes one 10-inch cake; serves 12 to 14

1 recipe Angel Food Cake, baked and cooled (page 34)

5 cups whole strawberries, stemmed and sliced

3 to 4 tablespoons sugar

½ teaspoon freshly squeezed lemon juice

1. Have the cake on a serving platter, ready to use.

2. Stir together half the berries in a medium-sized mixing bowl with 3 tablespoons sugar and the lemon juice. Allow to sit for 10 minutes until the juices begin to exude. Mash with a potato masher and stir in the remaining sliced berries. Taste and add additional sugar if needed. The fruit mixture may be made up to 6 hours ahead; refrigerate in an airtight container until needed.

3. Shortly before serving, slice the cake in half horizontally using a serrated knife with a sawing motion. Spoon half of the berries and their juices evenly over the bottom cake layer. Set the top layer in place and spoon the remaining berries and juices evenly over it. Allow the cake to sit for 10 minutes before serving, for the juices to seep through the cake. Serve immediately.

Applesauce-Raisin-Walnut Spice Cake

This cake has an old-fashioned appeal. The applesauce lends moistness and flavor, the spices are prominent, and the crumb is firm—the cake slices very easily. My Nana always said the applesauce should be hot; I don't know why, but it works! If you prefer a sweeter frosting, use Seven-Minute Frosting (page 45).

Makes one 9-inch round cake; serves 10 to 12

3½ cups all-purpose flour

2 teaspoons baking soda

½ teaspoon salt

1 cup toasted walnuts halves, chopped

½ cup dark raisins

½ cup golden raisins

1 cup (2 sticks) unsalted butter, at room temperature, cut into pieces

2 cups sugar

2 teaspoons ground cinnamon

1 teaspoon ground ginger

¼ teaspoon ground cloves

¼ teaspoon freshly grated nutmeg

2 large eggs, at room temperature

2 cups hot unsweetened applesauce

1 recipe Cream Cheese Frosting (page 52)

Cake decorations (optional)

1. Position a rack in the middle of the oven. Preheat the oven to 350°F. Coat the insides of two 9 × 2-inch round cake pans with nonstick cooking spray, line the bottoms with parchment rounds, then spray the parchment.

2. Whisk together the flour, baking soda, and salt in a large bowl to combine and aerate; toss in the nuts and dark and golden raisins; set aside.

3. In a large bowl, with an electric mixer on medium-high speed, beat the butter until creamy, about 2 minutes. Add the sugar gradually and beat until very light and fluffy, about 3 minutes, scraping down the bowl once or twice. Beat in the cinnamon, ginger, cloves, and nutmeg.

4. Beat in the eggs one at a time, scraping down after each addition and allowing each egg to be absorbed before continuing. Add the flour mixture in three additions, alternately with the applesauce. Begin and end with the flour and beat briefly until smooth. Divide the thick batter evenly between the pans and smooth the tops with an offset spatula.

5. Bake for 50 to 55 minutes, or until a toothpick inserted into the layers shows a few moist crumbs when removed.

6. Cool the pans on wire racks for 10 to 12 minutes. Unmold, peel off parchment, and place the layers directly on the racks to cool completely. The layers are ready to fill and frost. Alternatively, place the layers on cardboard rounds and double-wrap in plastic wrap; store at room temperature and assemble and serve within 24 hours.

7. Fill and frost with the prepared frosting and decorate as desired. The cake may be served immediately, or refrigerated overnight in a covered container. Bring to room temperature before serving.

Bananarama Cake

Banana fans, rejoice. The basic banana cake is filled and topped with fluffy meringue frosting, and has extra slices of banana nestled between the layers. The banana should be ripe but not mushy. It will be perfect the day it loses its green color, just begins to develop black speckles, and emits that enticing aroma.

Makes one 9-inch round cake; serves 10 to 12

1 recipe Banana Cake, baked and cooled (page 37)

1 recipe Fluffy Meringue Frosting (page 41)

1 large ripe but firm banana, sliced into ¼-inch rounds

Cake decorations (optional)

Have the cake layers and frosting ready to use. Place one cake layer on a serving platter. Spread a ¼-inch-thick layer of frosting evenly over the cake. Place half of the banana slices evenly over the frosting. Repeat with the second cake layer, frosting, and remaining bananas. Top with the last cake layer and cover the top and sides with the remaining frosting. Decorate as desired. The cake may be served immediately, or stored at room temperature overnight in a covered container.

Banana Split Cake

Banana, pineapple, strawberry, fudge (in the form of frosting), whipped cream, nuts, and—of course!—cherries on top make this cake reminiscent of a fountain shop sundae. A simple white cake allows the sundae flavors to shine. Serve with scoops of vanilla ice cream.

Makes one 9-inch round cake; serves 12 to 14

1 recipe White Cake, baked and cooled (page 32)

1 recipe Fudgy Chocolate Frosting (page 47)

1 large but firm banana, sliced into ⅛-inch rounds

½ cup pineapple preserves

¾ cup strawberry preserves

½ recipe Whipped Cream Frosting (page 52)

20 walnut halves

20 maraschino cherries

Pastry bag and coupler

Small star decorating tip such as Wilton or Ateco #18

1. Have the cake layers and chocolate frosting ready to use. With a thin, long-bladed knife, evenly slice each layer horizontally so there are four equal layers. Place one cake layer on a cardboard round, cut side up, and top with a very thin layer of chocolate frosting. Arrange the banana slices in an even single layer on top of the frosting. Place another cake layer on top, and spread on a thin, even layer of pineapple preserves. Place a third cake layer on top, and spread with a thin, even layer of strawberry preserves. Crown with the last cake layer, cut side down.

2. Frost the top and sides with chocolate frosting. The cake may be stored at room temperature overnight in a covered container.

3. Just before serving, use the pastry bag and tip to make whipped cream rosettes around the top outer edge of the cake. Nestle alternating walnuts and cherries in the rosettes.

Basket of Flowers Cake

Who wouldn't like to receive a big basket of flowers for their birthday? For the cake itself, choose white, yellow, or chocolate. The beige espresso buttercream lends a realistic straw basket look to the cake. The basketweave design takes time, but it isn't difficult. For the fresh flowers, use the birthday guy's or gal's favorite unsprayed edible flowers such as roses, pansies, bee balm, carnations, cornflowers, lavender, lilacs, or tulips. Note that when I say "edible," I mean they are safe, not necessarily tasty. More often than not, I remove the flowers before serving.

Makes one 9-inch round cake; serves 10 to 12

1 recipe White Cake (page 32), Yellow Cake (page 28), Quick 'n' Easy Yellow Cake (page 29), Dark Chocolate Cake (page 30), or Quick 'n' Easy Chocolate Cake (page 31), baked and cooled

1 standard batch Italian Meringue Buttercream, Espresso Variation (page 44)

Pastry bag and coupler

Ateco or Wilton tip #11

Fresh unsprayed edible flowers of choice

1. Have the cake layers and frosting ready to use. Fill and frost, creating a smooth crumb-coat. Chill the cake until the buttercream is firm, about 1 hour. Place the chilled cake on a serving platter.

2. Apply the basketweave pattern using the instructions, photos, and diagrams on page 14 for guidance. Use the same tip to pipe a bead border along the top and bottom edges of the cake. Chill until the buttercream is firm, about 1 hour.

3. The cake may be served immediately, or refrigerated overnight in a covered container. Bring to room temperature before serving.

4. Arrange the flowers on the cake just before serving, using the photo for inspiration, and remove them before slicing.

Baker's Tip

If you would like to use sprayed or non-edible flowers, place a round of parchment paper within the borders on the top of the cake. Arrange flowers on top of paper, taking care not to touch the cake; remove before serving. The photo shows tulips, sweet peas, and ranunculus.

Beginner Baker's Birthday Cake

Never made a cake before? This one is super easy and can be made with a couple of bowls, a whisk, and a rubber spatula; no baking experience is necessary. Read through the entire recipe before beginning so that you have a clear picture of the procedure. You will be rewarded with a buttery yellow cake with a deep chocolate glaze.

Makes one 9-inch round cake; serves 10 to 12

1 recipe Quick 'n' Easy Yellow Cake (page 29), baked and cooled

1 recipe Chocolate Ganache Glaze and Frosting (page 49), cooled to soft spreadable consistency

Candy decorations such as sprinkles, candy confetti, nonpareils, etc. (optional)

Baker's Tip Make sure the ganache is soft and spreadable, with a consistency between mayonnaise and peanut butter. If it is too stiff, give it 5-second bursts in the microwave until softened. If it is too soft, place the bowl over a larger bowl filled with ice and stir until thickened. Don't worry! Enjoy the process; I promise this will work!

1. Have the cake layers and frosting ready to use. Place one cake layer on a serving platter. Use the back of a large soup spoon to spread about 1 cup ganache frosting on top. Make sure to keep the spoon gliding on top of the frosting. If it touches the cake, it might bring up some crumbs.

2. Position the second cake layer on top of the first frosted layer. Place about 1 cup of frosting on top of the cake. Use the back of the spoon to gently spread the frosting all over the top of the cake. Glide the spoon around, pushing frosting toward the edges.

3. Apply the remaining frosting to the sides of the cake, spreading it around gently until the entire cake is covered. Finish by using the spoon to make pretty swirls here and there all over the cake. You do not have to make it smooth—the texture of the whirls and swirls is very attractive. The thing to remember is that the frosting can be manipulated until you get the result you want. Just keep at it and it will work beautifully. This cake needs no further embellishment. The cake may be served immediately, or stored at room temperature overnight in a covered container. Just add candles and you are ready to present your creation!

4. Here is an optional step. If this cake is for a child (or child-at-heart), a very easy way to make it more festive is to sprinkle candy decorations on top.

The Big Birthday Cake

I have been baking wedding cakes professionally for more than 20 years, so I have learned a thing or two about making cakes for crowds. Large cakes aren't difficult; they just take more planning, time, and refrigerator space, and some special equipment. This recipe is meant to serve as a guide when you need a cake for a lot of people.

To feed 50 to 60 guests, a two-tiered round cake will suffice; the bottom tier will be 12 inches across and the top tier 9 inches. Each tier will have two layers of cake. The terms "tier" and "layer" are not interchangeable and will be used differently throughout this guide. You'll have to make multiple batches of each cake recipe to make all four layers (see below).

Planning: To make this process as simple as possible, choose one flavor for the cake—white, yellow, or chocolate—from the Basics chapter. Each of the recipes yields a two-layer 9-inch cake, which will make up the top tier. For the 12-inch bottom tier, you need two 12-inch round layers. Each recipe for a two-layer 9-inch cake makes one 12-inch layer, so you will need to make two more batches of the batter and bake each in a 12 × 2-inch round pan. If you can borrow or don't mind buying two 12-inch pans, you can double the recipe and bake both 12-inch layers at once. But note that 9-inch cake recipes, if doubled, will not fit in a 5-quart stand mixer bowl; you will have to prepare the batter twice. The Quick 'n' Easy Yellow and Quick 'n' Easy Chocolate Cakes can be doubled and mixed by hand.

For the buttercream, I suggest the Italian Meringue Buttercream, because there are so many variations to choose from. Use a stand mixer to prepare two recipes of the larger batch (page 42). It can be made one month ahead and frozen.

The finished cake will be 14 to 16 inches across the bottom (depending on how you decorate it) and about 6 to 8 inches tall, so make sure you have room in the refrigerator.

Finally, give yourself enough time to bring the cake to room temperature before serving.

Timing: The buttercream and cake layers can be made up to a month in advance and frozen (see the section on Freezing Cake Layers). You will need to defrost the layers and buttercream overnight in the refrigerator, and bring the buttercream to warm room temperature, before assembling the cake.

Or make all the components at once, spreading out the preparations over 2 to 3 days. If the cake is to be presented on Saturday, make the buttercream and bake the cake layers on Thursday. Fill, frost, and decorate on Friday, and then refrigerate the cake overnight Friday to Saturday, which will help set the buttercream enough for transport, as very often these large cakes have to travel somewhere.

Equipment

Cake turntable
5-quart stand mixer
Assortment of icing spatulas
9-inch and 12-inch cardboard rounds
Pastry bag and coupler
Small star tip such as Ateco or Wilton #18
Four ¼-inch wooden dowels, at least 5 inches long

Dowels can be found at cake-decorating stores or in the hardware store. They will be submerged in the bottom tier and support the top tier.

You will also need a flat plate or platter, 14 to 16 inches across. It is not always easy to find one that is flat, so you might consider buying a "cake drum" from a cake-decorating or craft store (see Resources, page 154). This is a very sturdy board covered in silver or gold foil. Whatever you use must be sturdy enough to not flex under the weight of the cake and decorative enough to present to guests.

The other item that I strongly suggest (it only costs a few dollars) is a cake baking core. This is a metal tool the size and shape of a small paper drinking cup. It will draw heat to the center of the 12-inch tier,

encouraging even baking, which is critical with larger tiers. You will need two if you use two 12-inch pans at once.

Special Baking Instructions: When baking the 12-inch layers, use the baking core. Coat the core inside and out with nonstick cooking spray. Scrape the batter into the pan, reserving about ⅓ cup. Nestle the core in the center of the batter, open end up. Fill it with the reserved batter. Bake until a toothpick inserted into the layers (not inside the core) shows a few moist crumbs when removed. (Twelve-inch layers will bake for about 5 minutes longer than the 9-inch, so watch carefully.) Cool the pan on a wire rack for 10 to 12 minutes, then twist the core gently to remove it. Pop out the little "cakelet" inside. The 12-inch layer will have a hole in it where the baking core was. Fill it with the cakelet, cut to fit, height-wise. You now have a "whole" layer to fill and frost. No one will know the hole was there by the time you are done.

Assembly: At this point, the cake layers are baked and cooled, and the frosting is prepared and ready to use. Carefully read the section entitled How to Frost a Cake (page 10), especially Five Tips for Frosting Cakes (page 8). Below are some specifics.

1. Make sure the cake layers are level before filling and frosting them. Place the bottom layers of each size on their respective cardboard rounds. Prepare the tiers through the step where the crumb-coat is applied. Now chill them well.

2. Check the layers again to make sure they are level (this is important because when you stack the cakes, if they are not level, the entire creation will be off-kilter and unstable). Apply a final coat as smoothly as possible, building up any areas with buttercream that might be uneven, and chill well again.

3. Apply a large dab of frosting to the serving platter or cake drum and center the chilled 12-inch bottom tier; this buttercream will "glue" the cake to the platter. Now invert an empty 9-inch cake pan, center it over the 12-inch tier, and lightly press its rim onto the surface to make a mark. Lift the empty pan away. Submerge the four dowels straight down into the bottom tier, evenly spaced within the mark. Make a pen mark on each dowel where it meets the top of the cake. Remove the dowels and trim them along pen mark, using a sawing motion with a serrated knife. Reinsert them. They should be completely level with the tier's surface. Apply a large dollop of buttercream within the marked circle and spread it over the tops of the dowels. Use a large offset spatula to facilitate moving the 9-inch tier and place it within the mark on the 12-inch tier. It should be right over the dowels, which are now supporting the cardboard round under the 9-inch tier and therefore the tier itself. When the buttercream under the cardboard chills, it will act as "glue," affixing the top tier to the bottom.

4. Using the pastry bag and #18 decorator tip, make a simple shell or rosette border all along the bottom of the cake and along the base of the 9-inch tier. This will cover any of the cardboard that might be showing. Add any other buttercream decorations as desired. Chill cake until firm, at least 2 hours or preferably overnight if it is going to be transported. The thorough chilling will make it more stable. Bring to room temperature before serving.

Serving: Below is a chart to show you how to get the maximum number of servings per tier. Begin by separating the tiers; simply insert a spatula beneath the 9-inch cardboard and lift it off. You now have two separate cakes to cut as the diagram suggests.

Baker's Tip To embellish this cake easily, arrange the candles around the top of the bottom tier, and write "Happy Birthday" on the top tier with a contrasting color of buttercream. Fresh or crystallized flowers can be placed on the cake as well, if you like. Of course, any creative idea you come up with that is appropriate to the birthday person will work. Refer to the sections on birthday cake decorations for ideas.

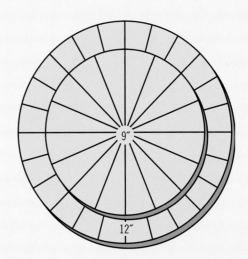

Yield if cut as shown: 56 servings (12-inch layer serves 40; 9-inch layer serves 16)

The Birthday Cake You Can Mail

Just because the whole family can't be around to sing "Happy Birthday" doesn't mean the birthday boy or girl doesn't deserve a homemade cake. This rich, buttery pound cake with two variations—mocha chip and citrus—can be safely sent by mail. The recipe includes packing directions to make sure the homemade cake gets to the lucky recipient fresh and undamaged. The packing materials can be found at any office supply store. Along with the cake you will be enclosing a small zipper-top bag filled with confectioners' sugar for sprinkling on right before serving. Remember to tuck in a birthday card and some candles.

**Makes one 10-inch Bundt cake;
serves 16**

Cake

2¼ cups sifted cake flour

1 teaspoon baking powder

¼ teaspoon salt

1½ cups (3 sticks) unsalted butter, at room temperature, cut into pieces

1¾ cups granulated sugar

1 tablespoon vanilla extract

6 large eggs, at room temperature

Mocha Version

2 teaspoons instant espresso dissolved in 2 teaspoons Kahlúa or brewed coffee

⅔ cup miniature semisweet chocolate morsels

Citrus Version

2 tablespoons finely grated lemon zest

2 tablespoons finely grated orange zest

¼ cup sifted confectioners' sugar

10-inch cardboard round

Small zipper-top plastic bag

Plastic wrap

Aluminum foil

Sturdy cardboard box large enough to fit cake with several inches of room on all sides

Packing peanuts

Birthday card

Candles

Wide packing tape

Black permanent marker

1. Position a rack in the middle of the oven. Preheat the oven to 325°F. Coat the insides of a Bundt pan with nonstick cooking spray, then completely dust with flour and shake out the excess.

2. Whisk the flour, baking powder, and salt together in a bowl to aerate and combine; set aside.

3. In a large bowl, with an electric mixer on medium-high speed, beat the butter until creamy, about 4 minutes. Add the granulated sugar gradually, beating until light and fluffy, about 4 minutes, scraping down the bowl once or twice. Beat in the vanilla. (For mocha, beat in the dissolved espresso at this point. For citrus, beat in the zests.) Beat in the eggs one at a time, scraping down after each addition and allowing each egg to be absorbed before continuing. Add the flour mixture in four additions, beating until smooth on low-medium speed after each addition. (For mocha, fold in the chocolate morsels at this point.) Scrape the batter into the prepared pan.

4. Bake the cake for 45 to 50 minutes, or until a wooden skewer inserted into the cake shows a few moist crumbs when removed. Cool the pan on a wire rack until almost completely cooled. Unmold and place the cake directly on the rack to cool completely. Place the cake on a cardboard round and wrap four times in plastic wrap, then in aluminum foil. Place the confectioners' sugar in the plastic bag and set aside.

5. Fill the box about one-quarter full with packing peanuts. Place the cake in center of the box, with the top of the cake facing up (there should be room on all sides). Pour more packing peanuts into the box to cover the cake and fill in the sides. Close the top and gently shake the box; the cake should barely move. If it does move, there are not enough packing peanuts. You can also fill up the space with crumpled newspaper. Reopen the box, fill if necessary, add the card, a package of candles, and the bag of confectioners' sugar. Close and seal with tape. Use the marker to write "Top" on the top of the box and "Keep Upright" on the sides with arrows pointing upward to the top.

Recipe continues on page 72

6. Do not mail on a Friday or Saturday. Also be aware of busy holidays when the mail might be slowed down. If you can afford overnight mailing options, use them (although you might have to repack the package in one of their special boxes). If the cake can arrive at its destination in 4 days or less, it will be absolutely fine.

Boston Cream Pie Birthday Cake

Pie tins were often used to bake cakes in the mid-nineteenth century, which is where the word "pie" in the name may have come from. The Parker House Hotel in Boston claims to have started serving this delectable dessert as early as 1856. In 1996, Boston Cream Pie was proclaimed the official Massachusetts state dessert; beating out toll-house cookies was an impressive feat. This "pie" masquerading as a cake features a sponge cake filled with vanilla pastry cream and topped with a glossy chocolate glaze. This moist cake manages to be rich and satisfying, yet light. My version is short in stature, but has just the right balance between cake, pastry cream, and glaze. If you want a taller cake, double the recipe for the sponge and bake it in two 9-inch pans.

Makes one 9-inch round cake; serves 8 to 10

1 recipe Hot Milk Sponge Cake (page 33), baked, cooled, and sliced in half horizontally

1 recipe Pastry Cream (page 53), chilled

Glaze

½ cup heavy cream

1 tablespoon light corn syrup

5 ounces semisweet chocolate, finely chopped

1. Have the cake layer and pastry cream ready to use.

2. For the glaze, place the cream and corn syrup in a large saucepan and bring to a boil over medium heat. Remove from the heat and immediately sprinkle the chocolate into cream. Cover and allow to sit for 5 minutes. The warm cream will melt the chocolate. Gently stir the ganache until smooth. If the chocolate is not melting, place the pan over a very low heat, stirring often, until melted, taking care not to burn chocolate.

3. Place one cake layer on a serving platter, cut side up. Spread the pastry cream evenly over the layer, then top with the second layer, cut side down.

4. Pour the chocolate glaze on top and gently spread it evenly and toward edges. Allow it to drip down sides.

5. Refrigerate the cake for at least 1 hour or up to 6 hours before serving. This cake is best served the same day.

Buttercream Roses Birthday Cake

Cakes at the many birthday parties of my childhood were topped with buttercream roses—and there was some fierce competition for those flowers! This single-layer 13 × 9-inch sheet-style cake is made in the flavor of the birthday person's choice, covered with vanilla buttercream, and decorated with a garden of roses. Tint the buttercream any color you like for the flowers. You will need a large flat platter for this cake. If you do not have one, use a 15 × 11-inch foil-covered cake base, which can be found at cake-decorating and some craft stores. (It is also called a cake drum.) Refer to page 14 for instructions on how to pipe roses and other frosting decorations.

Makes one 13 x 9-inch cake; serves 24 to 32

1 recipe batter for Quick 'n' Easy Yellow Cake (page 29) or Quick 'n' Easy Chocolate Cake (page 31)

1 standard batch Italian Meringue Buttercream, Vanilla Variation (page 44)

Gel coloring for roses and leaves (I used Wilton Burgundy and Moss Green)

Pastry bag and coupler

Ateco or Wilton tips #2, #8, #12, #21, #67, #101, and #104

1. Position a rack in the middle of the oven. Preheat the oven to 350°F. Coat the inside of a 13 × 9 × 2-inch cake pan with nonstick cooking spray, line the bottom with a parchment rectangle, then spray the parchment.

2. Prepare the batter of choice, scrape into the pan, and bake until a toothpick inserted into the cake shows a few moist crumbs when removed (timing will depend on the flavor selected; begin to test the cake at 20 to 25 minutes). Cool the pan on a wire rack until the cake is cool to the touch. Unmold onto a platter or a foil-covered cake base and peel off the parchment. Cool completely. The cake is ready to frost. Alternatively, double-wrap in plastic wrap; store at room temperature if assembling within 24 hours.

3. Smoothly frost the top and sides of the cake with vanilla buttercream. A small offset spatula is helpful in making the corners neat and smooth. Pipe a shell border on the top and bottom edges using tip #21.

4. Tint a larger quantity of the remaining frosting the color you want for the roses and tint a smaller amount green for leaves. The placement of the roses is up to you. Place the roses first, then the leaves (tip #67) and tendrils (tip #2) here and there if you like. Flower buds can be piped with tip #101. The cake may be served immediately, or refrigerated overnight in a covered container (if you can find one large enough). Bring to room temperature before serving.

Butter Pecan Cake with Brown Sugar Fudge Frosting

If you like an old-fashioned yellow cake with fudge frosting, but are looking for something a little bit different, then this is the cake to bake. The cake can be either the basic Yellow Cake or the Quick 'n' Easy Yellow Cake. The frosting is made like fudge candy, and you do need a candy thermometer; the use of dark brown sugar gives it a sophisticated and less-sweet edge. A stand mixer is best for making this thick frosting. Toasted pecans are scattered over the top of the cake, adding flavor and crunch. (If you sauté the pecans in 1 tablespoon of butter, the butter-pecan flavor will be accentuated.)

Makes one 9-inch round cake; serves 10 to 12

1 recipe Yellow Cake (page 28) or Quick 'n' Easy Yellow Cake (page 29), baked and cooled

Frosting

2 cups lightly packed dark brown sugar

1½ cups heavy cream

⅔ cup whole milk

6 ounces unsweetened chocolate, finely chopped

Pinch of salt

¼ cup (½ stick) unsalted butter, at room temperature, cut into pieces

¼ teaspoon vanilla extract

⅔ cup toasted pecans halves, chopped

1. Have the cake layers ready to use.

2. To make the frosting: Clip a candy thermometer to the side of a medium-size saucepan. Place the sugar, cream, milk, chocolate, and salt in the saucepan and stir to combine. Cook over medium-high heat, whisking occasionally, until the chocolate is melted. Bring to a boil and cook to 238°F, whisking from time to time. Scrape into the bowl of a stand mixer. Scatter the butter pieces on top and gently stir until the butter is incorporated. Allow to cool to room temperature; this could take 30 minutes or more. Stir occasionally to release heat. The frosting should be cool and form thick, satiny ribbons.

3. Beat the frosting with the flat paddle attachment on medium-high speed until the frosting just starts to lighten in color and additionally thicken. If the frosting does not look thick enough to spread, place the bowl over a larger bowl filled with ice until chilled before proceeding. Beat until the frosting is thick, creamy, and of spreading consistency. Beat in the vanilla.

4. Fill and frost the cake layers. Scatter the pecans over the top of the cake. The cake may be served immediately, or stored at room temperature overnight in a covered container.

Caramel-Walnut-Spice Birthday Cake

This velvety buttermilk cake is gently spiced with cinnamon, nutmeg, cardamom, cloves, and ginger—just enough to entice, not so much as to overwhelm. The caramel frosting, made with dark brown sugar, complements this cake perfectly; the caramel notes harmonize with the spices, and the sugary frosting texture contrasts with the tender cake. Note that the frosting sets up very quickly, so be prepared to frost the cake as soon as the frosting is ready and place the walnut halves on the top as you go, or they will not adhere.

Makes one 9-inch round cake; serve 10 to 12

1 recipe batter for Spice Cake (page 35)
¾ cup toasted walnuts halves, chopped
1 recipe Caramel Frosting (page 51)
16 walnut halves

1. Position a rack in the middle of the oven. Preheat the oven to 350°F. Prepare the spice cake batter according to the directions, adding ¾ cup chopped walnuts to the flour mixture. Bake and cool as directed.

2. Fill and frost the cake with the prepared frosting. While the frosting is still soft, arrange the walnut halves around the outer top edge of the cake. The cake may be served immediately, or stored at room temperature overnight in a covered container.

Chock-Full-of-Chips Cake

This recipe features the basic Yellow Cake speckled with miniature chocolate chips. Filled and frosted with a thick fudgy frosting and topped with a smattering of more chips, this is a chocolate chip–lover's dream. Kids adore this cake, although I have never had an adult turn down a piece.

Makes one 9-inch round cake; serves 10 to 12

1 recipe batter for Yellow Cake (page 28) or Quick 'n' Easy Yellow Cake (page 29)

¾ cup (plus 3 tablespoons, optional) miniature semisweet chocolate morsels

1 recipe Fudgy Chocolate Frosting (page 47)

1. Position a rack in the middle of the oven. Preheat the oven to 350ºF. Prepare the cake batter according to the directions, adding ¾ cup miniature chocolate morsels. Bake and cool as directed.

2. Have the frosting ready to use. Fill and frost the layers and decorate as desired. If you like, sprinkle 3 tablespoons chocolate morsels over the top of the cake. The cake may be served immediately, or stored at room temperature overnight in a covered container.

Chocolate Almond Apricot Cake with Chocolate Glaze

This elegant European-style torte is made with a dense, rich cake that contains a small bit of flour and a lot of ground almonds and chocolate in the batter. Baked in a deep springform pan, the cake is then split in half, filled with an apricot spread, and topped with a luscious chocolate glaze. I use an apricot spread made with 100 percent fruit. Look for it next to the jams and jellies in the supermarket. Apricot preserves can be used in a pinch, but the results will be sweeter. This is a fabulous cake to serve at an adult birthday party. It keeps well for three days.

Makes one 9-inch round cake; serves 12 to 14

Apricot Roses

12 dried whole apricots

Aluminum foil

Nonstick cooking spray

Rolling pin

Toothpicks

1. To make the apricot roses: Slice the whole apricots horizontally in half to create two round pieces. Put a piece of aluminum foil on the work surface, spray lightly with nonstick cooking spray, and place one apricot half on top. Spray another piece of aluminum foil with nonstick cooking spray and place that side down on top of the apricot. Use a rolling pin to flatten the apricot. It should be as thin as possible without tearing. Peel the apricot away from the foil and cut in half crosswise. Roll one half into a tight coil; this is the rose center. Flatten and press additional pieces around the center creating the petals; each petal should begin approximately at the mid-point of the petal before. Add as many as you like to create a smaller or larger rose. Gently unfurl the petals to "open" the rose a bit. Trim the bottom if necessary. If petals are not sticking to one another well, insert a toothpick horizontally through the pieces to hold them together. Repeat with the remaining apricots. These can be made 3 days in advance and stored at room temperature in an airtight container.

Recipe continues on page 80

Cake

2¾ cup toasted sliced almonds (natural or blanched)

¼ cup plus 1 tablespoon all-purpose flour

14 tablespoons (1¾ sticks) unsalted butter, at room temperature, cut into pieces

1 cup sugar

½ teaspoon vanilla extract

¼ teaspoon almond extract

8 large eggs, separated and at room temperature

7 ounces bittersweet or semisweet chocolate, melted and slightly cooled

½ cup apricot spread (100 percent fruit, no sugar added)

1 recipe Chocolate Ganache Glaze and Frosting (page 49)

2. To make the cake: Position a rack in the middle of the oven. Preheat the oven to 325°F. Coat the inside of a 9 × 3-inch round loose-bottom or springform pan with nonstick cooking spray. Line the bottom with a parchment round, then spray the parchment.

3. Place 1¾ cup of the nuts and the flour in a food processor fitted with the metal blade. Pulse on and off about 5 times, then run the processor until the nuts are very finely ground.

4. In a large bowl, with an electric mixer on medium-high speed, beat the butter until creamy, about 2 minutes. Add the sugar gradually and beat until very light and fluffy, about 3 minutes, scraping down the bowl once or twice. Beat in the vanilla and almond extracts. Beat in the egg yolks one at a time, scraping down after each addition and allowing each to be absorbed before continuing. Beat in the chocolate. Blend in the nut-flour mixture in two additions.

5. In a clean, grease-free bowl, with an electric mixer with clean beaters on low-medium speed, beat the egg whites until soft peaks form. Fold about one-quarter of the whites into the batter to lighten it; fold in remaining whites. Scrape the batter into the prepared pan.

6. Bake the cake for 50 to 55 minutes, or until a toothpick inserted into the cake shows a few moist crumbs when removed. Cool the pan on a wire rack for 10 minutes. Unmold the cake: Run an icing spatula around the sides of the cake to release it from the pan. Apply pressure out toward the pan, not in toward the cake, or you might accidentally shave off some of the cake's sides. If using a loose-bottom pan, press the bottom up to release. If using a springform, unlock and remove the pan sides. Invert the cake directly onto the rack, remove the bottom of the pan, peel off the parchment, and cool completely. (Keep the bottom of the cake as the top; it will be smooth and flat.) The cake is ready to fill and glaze. Alternatively, double-wrap in plastic wrap; store at room temperature if assembling within 24 hours.

7. Using a thin, long-bladed knife, slice the cake in half horizontally so there are two even halves. Place the bottom half, cut side up, on a cardboard round. Spread 6 tablespoons of the apricot spread evenly over the layer, then top with the second cake layer, cut side down (the original bottom of the cake should still be on top). Melt the remaining apricot spread in the microwave or on the stovetop and brush it all over the top and sides of the cake. There might be some crumbs; that's okay. Refrigerate briefly to set the apricot spread. Place the cake on a wire rack set over a clean pan.

8. Have the ganache loose and fluid, but not hot. Pour the glaze on top, gently spread it evenly toward the edges, and allow it to drip down the sides. Use a small icing spatula to spread it over the edges. Any excess that drips onto the pan can be reused.

9. Reserve about 10 almond slices. Place the remaining scant cup of almonds in bowl. Pick up the cake on the cardboard and hold it over the bowl of almonds with one hand. Apply the almonds with other hand, pressing them to the sides of the cake, covering it completely. Place the cake on a serving platter and arrange the roses (toothpicks removed) and extra almonds (to mimic leaves) on top of the cake. Refrigerate at least 1 hour, or until the glaze is set. The cake may be served immediately, or refrigerated overnight or up to 3 days, in a covered container. Bring to room temperature before serving.

Baker's Tip If you take advantage of the fact that you can make the apricot roses 3 days ahead, decorating the cake will be even easier.

Chocolate and Vanilla Cupcake Tower

Kids of all ages love cupcakes, probably because each person gets a cake—and an equal amount of frosting—of his or her own. The only decision is choosing between an all-chocolate or all-vanilla cupcake from this tower of treats. Two different colors of paper cupcake liners can help differentiate the cake flavors. Use a spring-loaded ice cream scoop to place the batter in each liner. This easy technique is quick, clean, and divides the batter evenly. Although cupcakes can be decorated in endless ways, a shower of candy confetti looks particularly festive on these. This tower uses a cupcake stand (such as the Wilton Cupcakes 'N More Dessert Stand; see Resources, page 154) or you can create one by stacking cake pedestals on top of one another.

Makes 24 cupcakes

Cupcakes

3 cups all-purpose flour

1 tablespoon baking powder

¼ teaspoon salt

1 cup (2 sticks) unsalted butter, at room temperature, cut into pieces

2 cups sugar

1 teaspoon vanilla extract

4 large eggs, at room temperature

1 cup whole milk, at room temperature

2 ounces unsweetened chocolate, melted and slightly cooled

24 paper liners in the color(s) of choice

1. To make the cupcakes: Position a rack in the middle of the oven. Preheat the oven to 350°F. Line two standard 12-cup muffin tins with paper liners.

2. Whisk together the flour, baking powder, and salt in a medium-size bowl to combine and aerate; set aside.

3. In a large bowl, with an electric mixer on medium-high speed, beat the butter until creamy, about 2 minutes. Add the sugar gradually and beat until very light and fluffy, about 3 minutes, scraping down the bowl once or twice. Beat in the vanilla.

4. Beat in the eggs one at a time, scraping down after each addition and allowing each egg to be absorbed before continuing. Add the flour mixture in three additions alternately with the milk. Begin and end with the flour and beat briefly until smooth. Remove half of the batter to a bowl and thoroughly stir in the melted chocolate.

5. Each flavor of batter will fill 12 liners. Divide the batter evenly among the liners and bake for 25 to 30 minutes (chocolate ones will take longer), or until a toothpick inserted into the cupcakes shows a few moist crumbs when removed. Cool the pans on wire racks for 5 minutes. Unmold and place the

Recipe continues on page 84

Frosting

1 recipe Confectioners' Sugar Frosting
(page 40)

3 ounces unsweetened chocolate, melted
and slightly cooled

Small candy confetti decorations

cupcakes directly on the racks to cool completely. The cupcakes are ready to decorate or store in airtight containers at room temperature. Decorate immediately or within 24 hours.

6. To frost: Have the frosting ready to use. Divide it in half and beat 3 ounces melted chocolate into one half. Use a small icing spatula to apply the chocolate frosting to the chocolate cupcakes and the vanilla frosting to the yellow cupcakes. Sprinkle with candy confetti while the frosting is still soft. Cupcakes are best served the same day they are baked, or store them overnight at room temperature in airtight containers.

Baker's Tip If you are stacking cake pedestals, do what professional prop stylists do. Buy Fun-Tak or similar reusable adhesive at the hardware store to "glue" the pedestals together. It will keep the pedestals from moving, and will remove cleanly when you are done.

Chocolate-Dipped Banana Birthday Cake

Have you ever had a frozen banana coated with chocolate and nuts? This cake features all of those kid- and adult-friendly flavors. Mini chocolate chips are added to the batter of the Banana Cake, which also contains chopped nuts. For the frosting, choose between the rich, sophisticated Sour Cream Chocolate Frosting, and the more traditional Fudgy Chocolate Frosting.

Makes one 9-inch round cake; serves 10 to 12

1 recipe batter for Banana Cake (page 37), made with only ½ cup pecans

1 cup miniature semisweet chocolate morsels

1 recipe Sour Cream Chocolate Frosting (page 50) or Fudgy Chocolate Frosting (page 47)

1. Position a rack in the middle of the oven. Preheat the oven to 350°F. Prepare the Banana Cake batter according to directions but use only ½ cup chopped pecans and add ½ cup miniature chocolate morsels to the flour mixture. Bake and cool as directed.

2. Fill and frost with the frosting of choice. While the frosting is still soft, sprinkle the remaining ½ cup morsels all over cake. Decorate as desired. The cake may be served immediately, or stored at room temperature overnight in a covered container.

Chocolate Extravaganza Birthday Cake

When I applied for my very first pastry chef position, I prepared a version of this cake: layers of chocolate cake, chocolate meringue, dark chocolate ganache, whipped chocolate ganache, and a cascade of large luscious chocolate curls on top. I got the job; enough said.

Makes one 9-inch round cake; serves 12 to 14

Chocolate Curls

1-pound block semisweet chocolate

Sharp 3-inch-diameter biscuit cutter

Whipped Chocolate Ganache

3 cups heavy cream

8 ounces bittersweet or semisweet chocolate, finely chopped

Chocolate Meringue

1 large egg white, at room temperature

Pinch of cream of tartar

⅓ cup sugar

1 tablespoon sifted Dutch-processed cocoa

1 recipe Dark Chocolate Cake (page 30) or Quick 'n' Easy Chocolate Cake (page 31), baked and cooled

½ recipe Chocolate Ganache Glaze and Frosting (page 49), at room temperature and spreadable

1. To make the chocolate curls: The chocolate should be one large block with a surface area at least 4 inches square. You will only use about half, but this size is easiest to work with. The chocolate needs to be very slightly warm. You can hold it between your palms for a few minutes, or you can place it in the microwave for 10 seconds at high power (depending on the size of chocolate and the strength of the microwave). Place the chocolate on the work surface (I place it on a piece of parchment) and hold it with one hand. Grasp the biscuit cutter firmly with the other hand. Beginning at the top of the piece of chocolate, hold the biscuit cutter nearly flat to the surface of the chocolate, ever so slightly angling it down near the top (this way, the top curve of the biscuit cutter is in contact with the chocolate). Applying pressure, firmly drag the cutter toward you. A curl should form and curl up over itself within the biscuit cutter. If the chocolate shatters, it is still too cold. If the chocolate is too soft, a curl will not form, either. Adjust the temperature and make curl after curl until you have used about half of the chocolate; you need to make enough to crown the top of the cake and/or cover the sides. Gently place the curls onto a plate in a single layer as you make them. These can be made several days before serving and stored in an airtight container at room temperature.

2. To make the whipped chocolate ganache: Place the cream in a large saucepan and bring to a boil over medium heat. Remove from the heat and immediately sprinkle the chocolate into the cream. Cover and allow to sit for 5 minutes. The heat of the cream should melt the chocolate. Gently stir until smooth. Pour into a mixing bowl, cover, and refrigerate at least 6 hours or overnight.

3. To make the chocolate meringue: Position a rack in the middle of the oven. Preheat the oven to 250°F. Line a baking sheet with parchment and trace an

8-inch circle. Flip the parchment over (you should be able to see the traced circle).

4. In a clean, grease-free bowl, whip the egg white with an electric mixer on low speed until frothy. Add the cream of tartar, increase the speed to high, and continue whipping until soft peaks form. Add the sugar gradually and continue to whip until stiff, but not dry, peaks form. Fold in the cocoa until thoroughly combined.

5. Use an offset spatula to spread an even layer of meringue within the traced circle. Take time to make it as round and level as possible.

6. Bake for 1½ hours, or until very dry and crisp. Cool the pan completely on a wire rack. The meringue disc is ready to use. Take care not to break the disc as you remove it from the parchment. It is best to place it on an 8-inch cardboard right away to protect it. The meringue may be stored in an airtight container until needed, up to 3 weeks.

7. To assemble the cake: Have all components ready to use. Beat the whipped chocolate ganache with an electric mixer until very soft peaks form; do not overbeat. Using a thin, long-bladed knife, slice the cake layers in half horizontally so there are four even layers. Place one layer, cut side up, on a cardboard round and spread with half of the chocolate ganache glaze. Top with the second cake layer, cut side down. Top with a layer of whipped ganache, the meringue, and then another layer of whipped ganache. Top with a third cake layer, cut side up, and spread with the remaining chocolate ganache glaze. Top with the last cake layer, cut side down. Cover the tops and sides with the remaining whipped ganache. Arrange the curls on top and press onto sides, if desired.

8. Refrigerate for at least 6 hours or overnight (this softens the meringue and brings all the textures together). Bring almost back to room temperature before serving.

Baker's Tip Making the chocolate curls can be tricky—it is all about temperature, so don't fret if it doesn't work at first. Don't be tempted to use bittersweet chocolate; it is usually too hard in texture to make curls easily, or at all. Also, take advantage of all the do-ahead steps in this recipe; it will be easier to assemble if you do. Note that the meringue layer is too small to make in a stand mixer. Use a hand-held mixer, or double the recipe, use your stand mixer, and make the extra into little round drop cookies.

Chocolate Soufflé Cake Roll

This cake is baked in a jellyroll pan and then rolled up around sweetened whipped cream. While it might sound somewhat plain, this version is ethereal and elegant in its simplicity. Some rolled cakes based on sponge cakes roll neatly and cleanly, but this chocolate cake does have a tendency to crack, as it is really more of a chocolate soufflé. The cracks can easily be forgiven because the taste and texture are so sublime. If you know to expect cracks, the cake's rusticity can be embraced—and a sprinkling of cocoa and/or confectioners' sugar on top will dress it up. You need a jellyroll pan that measures 16½ × 11¾ × 1 inches. (I measure mine across the bottom of the pan. Many pans are measured outer lip to outer lip and the dimensions will be different.)

Makes 1 approximately 12-inch roll; serves 12

Cake

5 ounces bittersweet chocolate, finely chopped

5 tablespoons water

6 large eggs, separated and at room temperature

¼ teaspoon cream of tartar

⅔ cup sugar

3 tablespoons Dutch-processed cocoa (plus 1 additional tablespoon, optional)

1 tablespoon confectioners' sugar (optional)

½ recipe Whipped Cream Frosting (page 52)

1. Position a rack in the middle of the oven. Preheat the oven to 350°F. Coat the inside of a jellyroll pan with nonstick cooking spray. Line the bottom with a parchment rectangle, then spray the parchment.

2. Melt the chocolate and water together in the microwave or the top of a double boiler and whisk until smooth; it will be thick. Cool slightly. Whisk in the egg yolks one at a time until the mixture is smooth and well blended.

3. In a clean, grease-free bowl, with an electric mixer on low-medium speed, beat the egg whites until foamy; add the cream of tartar and beat on high speed until soft peaks form. Gradually add the sugar and beat until stiff, but not dry, peaks form. Fold about one-quarter of the whites into the chocolate mixture to lighten it; fold in the remaining whites. Scrape the batter into the prepared pan and spread evenly with an offset spatula.

4. Bake for 10 to 12 minutes, or until a toothpick inserted into the cake shows a few moist crumbs when removed. Completely cool the pan on a wire rack. Place a large piece of parchment on a work surface and sprinkle evenly with the cocoa. Unmold the cake onto the cocoa-dusted parchment. Peel the parchment from the cake.

5. Have the frosting ready to use. Spread over the cake, leaving a ½-inch border at one short end. Use the cocoa-dusted parchment to facilitate rolling the

cake, starting at the short end opposite the end where you left a border. The first "turn" might be difficult and not very round. Just keep going; it rolls more smoothly as you go along. Use the parchment to protect the cake from your hands. Gently squeeze the finished roll into shape and mold it, if necessary, into an attractive "log." Keeping the parchment draped over the cake, transfer it to a serving platter. Chill for at least 1 hour to firm the roll.

6. Remove parchment and sprinkle remaining cocoa and/or confectioners' sugar, if desired, all over the top of the cake. The cake may be served immediately, or refrigerate overnight in a covered container.

Baker's Tip Don't worry when melting the chocolate and the water together this time. The proportions are such that the chocolate will not seize. You could also use coffee for a mocha-flavored cake. I use 70 percent cacao bittersweet chocolate such as Valrhona Guanaja. Different chocolates will definitely give different results; try different brands and percentages to see which ones you prefer.

Coco-licious Cake

This chocolate cake features cocoa in the batter. Half of the frosting is left white, and half is chocolate. Marbled together on the cake, it is a sophisticated twist on a homespun approach.

Makes one 9-inch round cake; serves 10 to 12

Cake

3 cups sifted cake flour

1 cup sifted natural cocoa

1½ teaspoons baking soda

1 teaspoon salt

1 cup plus 2 tablespoons (2¼ sticks) unsalted butter, at room temperature

1⅓ cups granulated sugar

1⅓ cups lightly packed light brown sugar

1½ teaspoons vanilla extract

3 large eggs, at room temperature

Scant 2 cups water or coffee, at room temperature

1 recipe Fluffy Meringue Frosting (page 41)

2 ounces unsweetened chocolate, melted and cooled

1. Position a rack in the middle of the oven. Preheat the oven to 350°F. Coat the insides of two 9 × 2-inch round cake pans with nonstick cooking spray, line the bottoms with parchment rounds, then spray the parchment.

2. Whisk together the flour, cocoa, baking soda, and salt in a medium-size bowl to combine and aerate; set aside.

3. In a large bowl, with an electric mixer on medium-high speed, beat the butter until creamy, about 2 minutes. Add the sugars gradually and beat until very light and fluffy, about 3 minutes, scraping down the bowl once or twice. Beat in the vanilla.

4. Beat in the eggs one at a time, scraping down after each addition and allowing each egg to be absorbed before continuing. Add the flour mixture in three additions, alternately with the water. Begin and end with the flour and beat briefly until smooth. Divide the batter evenly between the pans and smooth the tops with an offset spatula.

5. Bake for 45 to 50 minutes, or until a toothpick inserted into the layers shows a few moist crumbs when removed. The layers might have slightly domed tops, and will have begun to come away from the sides of the pans. Cool the pans on wire racks for 8 to 10 minutes. Unmold, peel off the parchment, and place the layers directly on the racks to cool completely. The layers are ready to fill and frost. Alternatively, place the layers on cardboard rounds and double-wrap each layer in plastic wrap; store at room temperature if assembling within 24 hours.

6. Have the frosting ready to use. Divide in half and beat the melted chocolate into one half. Apply large dollops of frosting here and there on the cake. Use an icing spatula to spread and marbleize the frosting. The cake may be served immediately, or stored at room temperature overnight in a covered container.

Coconut Rum Cake

This large, impressive cake combines an old-fashioned moist coconut cake with the flavor of gold rum. If you want to make the cake family friendly, leave out the alcohol. Pure coconut milk (not cream of coconut) is used in place of the whole milk in the basic Yellow Cake, and coconut is added to the batter. The cake layers are brushed with coconut-rum syrup and the whole cake is enrobed with Seven-Minute Frosting and more coconut. For a pretty feminine touch, wrap the cake with a ribbon tied in a bow. The thorough coating of coconut prevents the ribbon from sticking to the cake.

**Makes one 9-inch round cake;
serves 12 to 14**

Cake

1 recipe batter for basic Yellow Cake (page 28) made with 1 cup coconut milk in place of the whole milk

1 cup sweetened flaked or shredded coconut

Soaking Syrup

½ cup coconut milk

¼ cup sugar

3 tablespoons gold rum (or more or less to taste) such as Mount Gay Eclipse

Frosting and Decorating

1 recipe Seven-Minute Frosting (page 45)

2½ cups sweetened flaked or shredded coconut

1 yard 1½- to 2-inch ribbon (optional)

1. Position a rack in the middle of the oven. Preheat the oven to 350°F. Prepare the basic Yellow Cake batter using coconut milk in place of whole milk. Stir 1 cup coconut into the batter. Scrape the batter evenly into the prepared pans.

2. Bake for 25 to 30 minutes, or until a toothpick inserted into the layers shows a few moist crumbs when removed.

3. To make the soaking syrup: While the layers are baking, place the coconut milk and sugar in small saucepan; stir to combine. Bring to a simmer over medium-high heat and simmer until reduced by half. Stir in the rum, if using. Keep warm.

4. When the layers are done, place the pans on wire racks and immediately poke the layers all over with a bamboo skewer. Brush the layers evenly and equally with the warm soaking syrup. Cool completely in pans. Unmold and peel off the parchment. The layers are ready to fill and frost. Alternatively, place the layers on cardboard rounds and double-wrap in plastic wrap; store at room temperature and assemble and serve within 24 hours.

5. For the frosting: Have the frosting ready to use. Place the coconut in the bowl. Fill and frost the cake somewhat smoothly with the frosting (make sure the cake is on a cardboard round to make next step easier).

Recipe continues on page 94

6. To apply the coconut: Pick up the cake on the cardboard and hold it over a bowl of coconut with one hand. Apply the coconut with the other hand, pressing it to the top and sides of the cake, covering it completely. The cake may be served immediately, or stored at room temperature overnight in a covered container. If desired, wrap and tie the ribbon around the cake right before presenting, but remove before serving.

Baker's Tip Pure, unsweetened coconut milk can be found in Asian markets and the international aisle of supermarkets. It has no sugar added. Cream of coconut cannot be substituted.

Confetti 'n' Sprinkles Cake

I live in New England, where we call sprinkles "jimmies." Whatever you call them, this festive white cake has multicolored sprinkles stirred throughout the batter; they don't add any texture, but they do add specks of color. The layers are filled and frosted with a billowy white frosting and then covered with confetti-like candies. This cake is ideal for a child's birthday party at home or at school. Don't use brown or chocolate sprinkles; they make unattractive dark spots in the cake.

Makes one 9-inch round cake; serves 10 to 12

1 recipe batter for White Cake (page 32)

¼ cup plus 2 tablespoons multicolored sprinkles

1 recipe Fluffy Meringue (page 41) or Seven-Minute Frosting (page 45)

1. Position a rack in the middle of the oven. Preheat the oven to 350°F. Fold ¼ cup sprinkles into the batter. Bake and cool as directed.

2. Have the frosting ready to use. Fill and frost with the cake. Scatter the remaining sprinkles all over the top of the cake. The cake may be served immediately, or stored at room temperature overnight in a covered container.

Espresso Hazelnut Dacquoise

This elegant cake is all about the contrast of the crunchy, nutty dacquoise, which is a meringue made with ground nuts, and the silky smooth espresso buttercream. The perfect ending to an adult birthday party, this cake may be short in stature as far as birthday cakes go, but it is sophisticated, unique, and one of my favorites.

Makes one 8-inch round cake; serves 12 to 14

Dacquoise

¾ cup skinned, toasted hazelnuts

1½ tablespoons all-purpose flour

8 large egg whites, at room temperature

¾ teaspoon cream of tartar

2 cups sugar

1½ teaspoons almond extract

8 ounces bittersweet chocolate, finely chopped

1 standard batch Italian Meringue Buttercream, Espresso Variation (page 44)

Pastry bag and coupler

Ateco or Wilton tip #20

1. Position the racks in the upper and lower thirds of the oven. Preheat the oven to 250°F. Line two baking sheets with parchment and trace two 8-inch circles on one piece of paper and one 8-inch circle on the other. Flip the parchment over (you should be able to see the traced circles).

2. Place the nuts and flour in a food processor fitted with a metal blade. Pulse on and off about 5 times, then process until the nuts are very finely ground but still fluffy.

3. In a clean, grease-free bowl, whip the egg whites with an electric mixer on low speed until frothy. Add the cream of tartar, increase the speed to high, and continue whipping until soft peaks form. Add the sugar gradually and continue to whip until stiff, but not dry, peaks form. Beat in the almond extract. Fold in the ground nuts.

4. Using an offset spatula, spread an even ½-inch layer of dacquoise within the traced circles. Take time to make these as round and level as possible. There will be extra dacquoise leftover, which you should spread here and there outside the borders of the circles; this will eventually be crushed to apply to sides of the cake during assembly, so the shapes aren't important.

5. Bake for 1½ hours, or until very dry and crisp. The dacquoise may be very light brown. Cool the pans completely on wire racks. The dacquoise is ready to use. Take care not to break the round discs as you remove them from the parchment. It is best to place them on 8-inch cardboard rounds right away to protect them. The freeform pieces can be stored as is. The dacquoise may be stored in an airtight container until needed, up to 3 weeks.

Recipe continues on page 98

6. Melt the chocolate in the top of a double boiler or in the microwave. Spread the chocolate smoothly on the bottom of each disc using an offset spatula. Set aside, chocolate side up, at room temperature for chocolate to harden, or refrigerate briefly, about 5 minutes, to set chocolate. Meanwhile, crush the extra dacquoise pieces by hand into small pieces; some will be powdery and some should be up to about ¼-inch nuggets. Place the crushed dacquoise in a bowl.

7. Have the buttercream ready to use. Affix one dacquoise disc, chocolate side up, to a cardboard round with a dab of buttercream. Spread a ½-inch layer of buttercream all over disc. Top with second disc, chocolate side up, and top with ½-inch layer of buttercream. Place the last disc chocolate side down on the buttercream. Frost the top and sides with more buttercream, making the top very smooth and the sides fairly thick.

8. To apply the crushed dacquoise: Pick up the cake on the cardboard and hold it over the bowl of crushed dacquoise with one hand, and apply dacquoise with other. Place the cake on a serving platter. Pipe a shell or rosette border on the top and bottom edges, if desired. Chill until the buttercream is firm, about 1 hour. The cake may be served immediately, or refrigerated overnight in a covered container. Bring to room temperature before serving.

Baker's Tip If, after baking, the dacquoise circles have lost some of their roundness, you can trim them carefully with a sharp knife. The rounder they are, the easier the cake will be to assemble and decorate—and the better it will look when done.

German Chocolate Cake

While researching this book, I spoke with several people who said no birthday would be complete without this cake. Chocolate layers are filled and topped with a sweet coconut-pecan frosting. The name of the cake comes from a sweet chocolate bar developed for Baker's Chocolate Company by Sam German in the mid-1800s. It was originally called German's Chocolate Cake because the cake was made with his chocolate. The traditional version has three layers and is made with sweet chocolate and buttermilk. If you are short on time, use the Quick 'n' Easy Chocolate Cake (page 31) with its two layers. Whether two or three layers, the filling is only used between the layers and on top of the cake, leaving the sides exposed; it gives a great ratio of the cake to frosting.

Makes one 9-inch round cake; serves 12 to 14

Cake

4 ounces semisweet or Baker's German Sweet chocolate, finely chopped

½ cup water

1 cup buttermilk

2¼ cups all-purpose flour

1 teaspoon baking soda

½ teaspoon salt

1 cup (2 sticks) unsalted butter, at room temperature, cut into pieces

1½ cups sugar

4 large eggs, at room temperature

1½ teaspoons vanilla extract

1. To make the cake: Position the racks in the upper and lower thirds of the oven (you'll use both racks). Preheat the oven to 350°F. Coat the insides of three 9 × 2-inch round cake pans with nonstick cooking spray, line the bottoms with parchment rounds, then spray the parchment.

2. Melt the chocolate and water together in the microwave or the top of a double boiler and whisk until smooth. Cool to room temperature. Whisk together with the buttermilk; set aside.

3. Whisk together the flour, baking soda, and salt in a medium-size bowl to combine and aerate; set aside.

4. In a large bowl, with an electric mixer on medium-high speed, beat the butter until creamy, about 2 minutes. Add the sugar gradually and beat until very light and fluffy, about 3 minutes, scraping down the bowl once or twice. Beat in the vanilla.

5. Beat in the eggs one at a time, scraping down after each addition and allowing each egg to be absorbed before continuing. Add the flour mixture in three additions, alternately with the chocolate-buttermilk mixture. Begin and end with the flour and beat briefly until smooth. Divide the batter evenly among the pans and smooth the tops with an offset spatula.

Recipe continues on page 100

Frosting

1⅓ cups evaporated milk

1⅓ cups sugar

4 large egg yolks, at room temperature

10 tablespoons (1¼ sticks) unsalted butter, at room temperature, cut into pieces

1½ teaspoons vanilla extract

2 cups sweetened flaked or shredded coconut

1⅓ cups toasted pecan halves, chopped

6. Bake for 20 to 25 minutes, or until a toothpick inserted into the layers shows a few moist crumbs when removed. The layers will have begun to come away from the sides of the pans. Cool the pans on wire racks for 8 to 10 minutes. Unmold, peel off the parchment, and place the layers directly on the racks to cool completely. The layers are ready to fill and frost. Alternatively, place the layers on cardboard rounds and double-wrap in plastic wrap; store at room temperature if assembling within 24 hours.

7. To make the frosting: Place the evaporated milk and sugar in large saucepan and whisk to combine. Whisk in the egg yolks and butter. Gently cook over medium heat until the mixture reaches a simmer. Cook for about 8 minutes, whisking frequently, until it slightly darkens and thickens. Remove from heat and stir in the coconut and pecans. Cool, stirring occasionally to release heat, until just warm to the touch and thickened.

8. Place one cake layer on a serving platter and top with a thick layer of frosting. Top with the second layer and frost just the top. Finish with the last cake layer and top with the remaining frosting. Allow to cool completely, which will set the frosting. The cake may be served immediately, or stored at room temperature overnight in a covered container.

Gilded Candy Roses Birthday Cake

Candy roses, made with your color choice of Wilton Candy Melts and then embellished with edible gold powder, make this cake truly spectacular. These roses can be used to crown any cake you like, but because they are so exquisite, I think it is best to make the cake elegant and sophisticated as well. Use the Italian Meringue Buttercream for this cake, as it has the most refined texture and flavor. Note that while it does take time to make the roses, they can be made up to one month ahead. You can see these roses in the photo on page 107. The gold powder can be ordered from Beryl's (see Resources, page 154).

***Makes one 9-inch round cake;
serves 10 to 12***

1 recipe Candy Plastic (page 55), made with white Candy Melts

Edible gold powder

Vodka

Small artist's brush

1 finished baked, cooled, filled, and frosted 9-inch cake of choice, frosted with Italian Meringue Buttercream, Vanilla or Liqueur Variation (page 44)

1. Make an assortment of different size roses and leaves and a few tendrils, as described on page 20. At a minimum, make 3 large roses, 4 medium, and 4 small, and at least 2 leaves of appropriate size per rose.

2. Place about 1 teaspoon gold powder in a small bowl and add vodka drop by drop, stirring with the brush, until it forms a paint consistency. Paint the edges of the rose petals as shown. For the leaves you can paint the edges or mimic the paths of the veins. Let dry.

3. Arrange the roses as desired on top of the cake as well as along the bottom edge. Nestle the base of the roses into the buttercream, then arrange leaves here and there to cover the insertion point as well as add further detail. Tendrils can be placed coming out from under the leaves as well. The cake is ready to serve.

> **Baker's Tip**
> You can create a different kind of look by painting the edge of the roses with plain vodka and then sprinkling them with edible glitter or colored sugars. Try using similar or contrasting colors for different effects.

Hairy Caterpillar Cupcake Cake

The color of the "hair"—tinted coconut—can be the birthday person's favorite color. Twelve cupcakes are arranged into a long caterpillar, so you will need a very large platter or a large piece of corrugated cardboard covered in foil to support this critter. To get the cupcakes to look round, the buttercream needs to be soft enough be workable but still firm enough so that it sticks to the cupcakes as you roll them around. Once the cupcakes are rolled in the coconut, they will be quite round. Twelve additional cupcakes are baked in paper liners and served on the side. Cupcakes dry out quickly, so take care not to over bake them. These are best served the same day they are baked.

Makes 24 cupcakes

1 recipe batter for Yellow Cake (page 28), Quick 'n' Easy Yellow Cake (page 29), or White Cake (page 32)

6 cups sweetened shredded coconut

Gel or paste food coloring, green or color of choice

1 large batch Italian Meringue Buttercream, Vanilla Variation (page 44)

Assorted candies and pretzels (see photo for inspiration) such as very small straight pretzel sticks for antennae, licorice whip for mouth, and small round candies for eyes

1. Position the racks in the upper and lower thirds of the oven (you'll use both racks). Preheat the oven to 350°F. Coat the insides of one standard 12-cup muffin tin with nonstick cooking spray. Line another standard 12-cup muffin tin with decorative fluted paper liners. Prepare the batter of choice. Fill the wells about three-quarters full with batter and bake until a toothpick inserted into the cupcakes shows a few moist crumbs when removed. The exact timing will vary depending on the recipe selected, but cupcakes bake quickly so begin testing at 15 minutes. Cool the pans on a wire rack for 5 minutes, then unmold the cupcakes and place them directly on the rack to cool completely.

2. For the hair, place the coconut in a large bowl. Add ⅛ teaspoon coloring and stir and toss the coconut with a metal spoon (it will dye wooden implements) until the color is distributed throughout. Add more color, if necessary, to get the effect you want.

3. Have the frosting ready to use; it should be as soft as mayonnaise. Line a jellyroll pan with aluminum foil; set aside. Place about 2 cups of soft buttercream in a small bowl. Using the 12 paperless cupcakes, literally roll a cupcake around in the buttercream. This is not an exact science—and it is somewhat messy! You are just trying to get a fairly even coating of buttercream all around the cupcake. Use your fingertips or two spoons to push the cupcake around on the surface of the buttercream. Remove the cupcake from the buttercream and immediately roll it in the coconut. The cupcake will

take on a round shape. Keep rolling it until it is completely covered. Transfer to the prepared jellyroll pan. Repeat with 11 more cupcakes, replenishing buttercream as you go. (The reason for using a small amount at a time is so that if a cupcake falls apart and produces a lot of crumbs, you will not ruin all of the buttercream.)

4. Arrange the cupcakes end-to-end on a serving platter. I find a slightly curving, wiggly shape is best. Insert pretzels for antennae, and create eyes and mouth as desired using candies. Legs can also be made using short pieces of licorice. Chill until the buttercream firms, at least 1 hour. Bring back to room temperature before serving.

5. Spread the remaining buttercream on the remaining cupcakes and top with coconut. Serve on a platter alongside the "caterpillar."

Heart of Gold Chocolate Raspberry Cake

This versatile flourless chocolate cake, covered with a dark chocolate glaze, has many things going for it besides its intense chocolate flavor. Once baked, it can be refrigerated for a few days or frozen for several weeks. You can bake it in an 8-inch heart-shaped or round pan; the baking times will be the same. If raspberries are out of season, omit them. No gold powder? No problem; this dessert is dramatic enough without it. You do, however, have to start making the cake a day ahead of serving it. A little lightly sweetened whipped cream on the side cuts the richness of the cake; you can use the Whipped Cream Frosting (page 52). The gold powder can be ordered from Beryl's (see Resources, page 154) or other well-stocked cake-decorating stores. While this cake sounds extra fancy—and it looks it—it is surprisingly easy to make. For an optional embellishment, add candy plastic roses (page 20), as shown in the photograph.

Makes one 8-inch heart-shaped or round cake; serves 14

Cake

6 large eggs, at room temperature

1 pound semisweet chocolate, finely chopped

1 cup (2 sticks) unsalted butter, at room temperature, cut into pieces

⅔ cup firm, dry, fresh raspberries

Glaze

¾ cup heavy cream

7½ ounces semisweet chocolate, finely chopped

1 tablespoon raspberry liqueur such as Chambord, framboise, or schnapps (optional)

Edible gold powder

Vodka

Small artist's brush

1. Position a rack in the middle of the oven. Preheat the oven to 375ºF. Using an 8 × 2-inch heart-shaped cake pan as a stencil, trace a heart outline on a larger cardboard round and cut out the heart to use as a base for the cake. Coat the inside of the pan with nonstick cooking spray, line the bottom with a parchment heart, then spray the parchment.

2. Place the eggs, in their shells, in a bowl filled with hot tap water for 5 minutes. (Warming the eggs ensures maximum volume when they are whipped.)

3. Melt the chocolate and butter in the top of a double boiler or the microwave. Stir until smooth, then cool slightly.

4. Meanwhile, crack the eggs into a bowl and beat with an electric mixer on high speed for 3 to 5 minutes, until tripled in volume, pale yellow, and thick enough to hold a very soft peak.

5. Add about one-quarter of the egg mixture to the cooled chocolate. Gently whisk by hand to combine. (It's okay if streaks of egg remain.) Add the remaining eggs and fold in, first using the whisk, then finishing with a large rubber spatula. The batter will deflate a bit, but try to retain as much volume as possible. The mixture will look like chocolate mousse. Scrape the batter into the prepared pan and level with a small offset spatula.

6. Scatter the raspberries evenly over the surface. Use the blunt end of a chopstick or your finger, and poke the raspberries into the batter one at a time. You want to submerge them, at different levels, and they should not touch the sides of the pan or each other. (When the cake is unmolded, you should not see the berries at all.) Place the pan in a larger pan filled with 1 inch of hot water.

7. Bake for 14 to 18 minutes. The surface will look dull. If you tilt the pan slightly, the edges of the cake will come away from the sides of the pan. Both of those visuals are important and really the only way to tell that it is done. It will still be very soft, like a pudding. Don't fret.

8. Cool the pan completely on a wire rack. Wrap with plastic wrap and refrigerate overnight. (The cake may be frozen up to 1 week; if made without berries it may be frozen for 1 month. Defrost in the refrigerator overnight.)

9. To unmold, unwrap the pan, flip it over (the cake will not fall out) and allow hot tap water to run all over the bottom of the pan. The warmth from the water should loosen the cake from the sides and bottom of the pan. Flip the pan back with the open side up. Warm an icing spatula under hot running water and blot dry. Run the spatula around the sides of the cake to release it from the pan. Apply pressure out toward the pan, not in toward the cake, or you might accidentally shave off some of the cake's side. Place the cardboard on top of the cake and hold it in place. Flip the cake. Very firmly jiggle the pan back and forth; you are trying to get the cake to release its surface tension with the pan. You should feel the cake begin to slip out. If it doesn't, repeat the warm water and jiggling steps. When it starts to slide down and out of the pan, lower the cardboard to the table and gently lift off the pan. Peel off the parchment. The cake is ready to glaze.

10. To make the glaze: Place the cream in a large saucepan and bring to a boil over medium heat. Remove from the heat and immediately sprinkle the chocolate into the cream. Cover and allow to sit for 5 minutes. The heat of the cream should melt the chocolate. Gently stir the ganache until smooth. Stir in the liqueur, if using. If the

chocolate is not melting, place over a very low heat, stirring often, until melted, taking care not to burn the chocolate.

11. Place the cake on a wire rack set over a clean pan. Spread the glaze on top, gently spread it evenly and toward the edges, and allow it to drip down the sides. Use a small icing spatula to spread it over the edges. Any excess that drips onto the pan can be reused. Place the cake on a serving platter and refrigerate at least 1 hour, or until the glaze is set.

12. Place about ½ teaspoon gold powder in a small bowl. Add vodka a drop at a time and stir with the brush until it is of paint consistency. "Paint" birthday wishes on top of the chilled glaze. The cake may be served immediately, or refrigerated up to 3 days in a covered container. Serve slices of the cake cold; it is best sliced with a thin-bladed knife dipped in hot water between cuts.

Baker's Tip This is one time I suggest cutting out a cardboard base, because heart-shaped ones are not usually available.

Hummingbird Cake with Fresh Fruit

A favorite in the southern United States, this cake is loaded with pineapple, nuts, and bananas, making it moist, flavorful, and a good keeper. Baked in a Bundt pan and covered with cream cheese frosting, the cake makes for an unusual but welcome birthday cake. To gild the lily, I fill the center of the cake with fresh fruit, making it a perfect choice for a fruit lover.

Makes one 10-inch Bundt cake; serves 16

3 cups all-purpose flour

2 cups sugar

1 teaspoon baking soda

1 teaspoon cinnamon

1 teaspoon salt

1⅓ cups vegetable oil such as canola or safflower

3 large eggs, at room temperature

2 large ripe bananas, sliced into ½-inch rounds

1½ cups toasted pecans halves, chopped

1 cup canned crushed pineapple, lightly drained

1½ teaspoons vanilla extract

1 recipe Cream Cheese Frosting (page 52)

3 cups fresh fruit such as quartered strawberries, whole raspberries, or peeled and sliced peaches or nectarines

1. Position a rack in the middle of the oven. Preheat the oven to 350°F. Coat the inside of a Bundt pan with nonstick cooking spray, then completely dust with flour and shake out the excess.

2. Whisk together the flour, sugar, baking soda, cinnamon, and salt in a large bowl to combine and aerate; set aside.

3. Whisk together the oil and eggs until well blended in a medium-size bowl. Stir in the bananas, nuts, pineapple, and vanilla.

4. Pour the wet ingredients over the dry and stir until combined. The batter will be heavy; make sure you combine well and there are no pockets of flour left. Scrape into the prepared pan.

5. Bake for 55 minutes to 1 hour and 5 minutes, or until a wooden skewer inserted into the cake shows a few moist crumbs when removed. Cool the pan on a wire rack until almost completely cooled. Unmold and place the cake directly on the rack to cool completely. The cake is ready to frost. Alternatively, place the cake on a cardboard round and double-wrap in plastic wrap; store at room temperature and assemble within 24 hours.

6. Have the frosting ready to use. Cover the entire cake, top, sides, and inside the center with frosting. Make attractive but casual swirls here and there all over the cake with an icing spatula or the back of a spoon. The cake may be served immediately, or refrigerated overnight in a covered container. Bring to room temperature before serving.

7. Right before serving, fill the center of the cake with your fruit of choice, making sure there is a generous amount, mounding it in the center. If desired, individual pieces of fruit can be used to decorate the base of the cake as well; this works best with berries.

Baker's Tip Strawberries or raspberries can also be used as candleholders. A generous application of frosting will anchor the berries. For raspberries, use dry, firm berries and place them open side up around the top of the cake; insert candles gently so that each berry hugs the base of a candle; push the candles all the way into the cake. For strawberries, choose smaller berries, remove the stems and place stem-end down on top of the cake. Use a skewer to make a hole through the berry vertically, then insert a candle.

Ice Cream Birthday Cake

Count me in as one of those people who loves ice cream more than almost any other food. For folks like us, an ice cream birthday cake is the answer—and this one has three great features going for it. For starters, it is assembled with purchased ingredients, so no baking is required. Second, it takes about fifteen minutes to put together; and lastly, it can be varied endlessly. The cake is made up of three components: cookies, ice cream, and Chocolate Ganache Glaze and Frosting. One set of flavors is described below, but feel free to experiment. Use vanilla sandwich cookies, ginger cookies, oatmeal cookies, or chocolate chip cookies. Strawberry ice cream, butter pecan, or chocolate . . . you get the idea. The easiest way to get the ice cream into the pan is with a standard size ice cream scoop. Make sure the springform pan measures a full 9 inches across and 3 inches deep, or the amounts will not fit. If you have a smaller pan, use less ice cream for those layers and perhaps less ganache as well.

Makes one 9-inch round cake; serves 12 to 14

One 1-pound 2-ounce package chocolate creme sandwich cookies such as Oreos

5 cups premium coffee ice cream, slightly softened

5 cups premium vanilla ice cream, slightly softened

½ recipe Chocolate Ganache Glaze and Frosting (page 49)

1. Coat the inside of a 9 × 3-inch round springform pan with nonstick cooking spray. Place the whole cookies flat in the pan to cover the bottom as efficiently as possible. There will be some holes, which is okay. Just pack the whole cookies in there as tightly as possible. Use an ice cream scoop to place large scoops of coffee ice cream all over the cookie layer. Use an offset spatula or the back of a sturdy spoon to press the ice cream down onto the cookies. You are not only trying to level the ice cream layer; you are also trying to press the ice cream into the little spaces between the cookies (if you are having trouble with this, just wait a minute or two for the ice cream to soften further).

2. Arrange another solid, single layer of cookies over the ice cream, then cover with a layer of the vanilla ice cream. Make sure you have at least ½ inch headroom left in the pan. Freeze the cake until the top layer of ice cream is solid, at least 1 hour.

3. Meanwhile, make the topping. Pour the warm (not hot) topping onto the center of the cake all at once. Quickly and gently spread it so that it covers the entire surface. Freeze again until solid, at least 2 hours or overnight. The

cake may be served immediately, softened slightly before slicing. Alternatively, it may be wrapped well in plastic wrap (still in the pan) and frozen for up to 4 days.

4. To unmold the cake: Warm an icing spatula under hot running water and shake dry. Run the spatula around the sides of the cake to help release it from the pan. Apply pressure out toward the pan, not in toward the cake, or you might accidentally shave off some of the cake's sides. Unlock the springform and remove the pan sides. Place on a serving platter.

Baker's Tip As mentioned in the headnote, don't limit the flavors to coffee and vanilla ice cream. One layer can be sorbet. For example, try chocolate creme sandwich cookies, vanilla ice cream, and raspberry sorbet, or soft chocolate chip cookies, vanilla ice cream and chocolate sorbet . . . this is a great recipe to plan and make with kids, as they can help pick out the flavors and help with the actual assembly.

Liqueured-Up Layer Cake with Vanilla Buttercream and Crystallized Flowers

While this cake begins with the basic Yellow Cake, the layers are flavored further and moistened by adding a liqueur or sweet alcohol such as amaretto, Cointreau, Grand Marnier, rum, fruit brandy, or eau-de-vie. The cake is then filled with Rich Egg Yolk Buttercream and frosted with vanilla Italian Meringue Buttercream. It is delicate yet flavorful, making it ideal for an elegant dinner party. You can make your own crystallized flowers (see page 19), or order the exquisite ones made by my friend Toni Elling from Meadowsweets (see Resources, page 154), which are pictured on page 17.

Makes one 9-inch round cake; serves 12 to 14

Syrup

¼ cup water

¼ cup sugar

¼ cup liqueur of choice

1 recipe Yellow Cake (page 28) or Quick 'n' Easy Yellow Cake (page 29), baked and cooled

½ recipe Rich Egg Yolk Buttercream, vanilla variation (page 46)

One-half standard batch Italian Meringue Buttercream, Vanilla Variation (page 44)

Pastry bag and coupler

Small star decorating tip such as Wilton or Ateco #16

About 12 crystallized flowers

1. To make the syrup: Combine the water and sugar in a small saucepan. Stir to wet the sugar thoroughly. Place the pan over medium heat and bring to a simmer. Cook for 1 minute, or until the sugar dissolves, swirling the pan once or twice. Remove from heat and cool to room temperature. The syrup is ready to use, or can be refrigerated in an airtight container for up to 1 month. Stir in the liqueur just before using.

2. Have the cake layers and frostings ready to use. Using a thin, long-bladed knife, horizontally slice each layer in half so that there are four equal layers. Place one cake layer, cut side up, on a cardboard round. Brush with the syrup and top with some buttercream. Top with another cake layer and repeat the sequence, ending with the last cake layer, cut side down, and a brush of syrup. Apply a crumb-coat of buttercream and chill well before applying a smooth final coat.

3. Using a pastry tip, make elongated reverse shell borders, top and bottom edge (see photo, page 12). The cake may be served immediately, or refrigerated overnight in a covered container. Bring to room temperature and decorate with the flowers right before serving.

Luscious Lemon-Blueberry Meringue Cake

Lemon meringue pie devotees will ask for this birthday cake every year. Lemon juice and zest perk up the buttery Yellow Cake batter. The cake is filled and topped with lemon curd. Then the entire cake is slathered with meringue and browned in the oven. It is dramatic looking and sure to please the lemon lover.

**Makes one 9-inch round cake;
serves 10 to 12**

1 recipe batter for Yellow Cake (page 28)

1 tablespoon freshly squeezed lemon juice

1 tablespoon finely grated lemon zest

¾ cup fresh blueberries

Meringue

5 large egg whites, at room temperature

¾ cup sugar

½ teaspoon vanilla extract

1 recipe Lemon Curd (page 54)

1. Position a rack in the middle of the oven. Preheat the oven to 350°F. Prepare the cake according to directions but beat in the lemon juice and zest when beating in the vanilla in the basic recipe. Fold the blueberries into the batter. Bake and cool as directed.

2. To make the meringue: Preheat the oven to 400°F. Combine the egg whites and sugar in a heatproof bowl and set over simmering water. Whisk to combine, and continue to whisk often as the mixture gently heats. After a few minutes, test some between your fingertips; the sugar should be dissolved, all grittiness should have disappeared, and the mixture should be very warm. Take care not to cook the egg whites.

3. Remove from the heat and beat with an electric mixer until thick, firm peaks form. Beat in the vanilla.

4. Fill and top the cake with the lemon curd. Do not apply any to the sides, just use as filling and topping. (I use about ½ cup lemon curd each filling and topping, in which case I have some left over.)

5. Place the cake, on a cardboard round, on a baking sheet. Cover completely with the meringue, making dramatic peaks going in various directions (see photo). Lightly brown in the oven, about 7 minutes (timing is less important than the look of the meringue; it should be lightly browned). Place on a serving platter. The cake may be served immediately, or stored at room temperature for up to 6 hours in a covered container.

Mocha 'Nana Birthday Cake

*Many of the birthday cakes in this book come from real families with real birthday cake histories.
My good friends Amy Wasserman, Scott Plotkin, and their daughter Lily Patrice Isabella Plotkin
enjoy this banana cake with mocha frosting at birthdays. It hails from Scott's side of the family;
they gave me a written copy from his grandmother. The title of the recipe refers both to his Nana
and the bananas. There are four generations enjoying this cake in their family tree—most
recently a 75th birthday as well as a fifth. Make sure you have a large serving platter, or use a
15 × 11-inch foil-covered cake base, which can be found at cake-decorating and some craft stores.*

**Makes one 13 x 9-inch cake;
serves 24 to 30**

1 recipe batter for Banana Cake
(page 37)

Frosting

1 tablespoon instant coffee or espresso
powder

1 tablespoon warm whole milk (plus
extra as needed)

4 cups sifted confectioners' sugar (plus
extra as needed)

½ cup (1 stick) unsalted butter, at room
temperature, cut into pieces

1 tablespoon natural or Dutch-processed
cocoa

1. Position a rack in the middle of the oven. Preheat the oven to 325°F. Coat the inside of a 13 × 9 × 2-inch cake pan with nonstick cooking spray, line the bottom with a parchment rectangle, then spray the parchment. Scrape the batter into the prepared pan and spread evenly with an offset spatula.

2. Bake for 55 minutes to 1 hour and 5 minutes, or until a toothpick inserted into the cake shows a few moist crumbs when removed. The cake will be tinged light golden brown. Cool the pan on a wire rack until cool to the touch. Unmold onto a platter or foil-covered cardboard and peel off the parchment. Cool completely. The cake is ready to frost. Alternatively, double-wrap in plastic wrap; store at room temperature if assembling within 24 hours.

3. To make the frosting: Dissolve the coffee in the milk; set aside. In a large bowl, with an electric mixer on medium-high speed, beat the butter until creamy, about 2 minutes. Add 1 cup of the sugar gradually, beating until light and fluffy, about 3 minutes, scraping down the bowl once or twice. Add the remaining sugar, coffee mixture, and cocoa, and beat on high speed until silky smooth. Adjust the texture with additional milk or confectioners' sugar, if necessary. The frosting is now ready to use.

4. Frost the top and sides of the cake, making simple swirls here and there. The cake may be served immediately, or stored overnight at room temperature in a covered container (if you have one large enough).

Mocha Toffee Crunch Cake

This is a big, important cake, perfect for significant milestone birthdays. Many of the components—the cake, the buttercream, and the ganache—can be made ahead. This cake elicits "ooohhhs and aaahhhs" and once guests taste it they will be clamoring for the recipe. My good friend Kerry Boyd requested a cake with these flavors for her fortieth birthday, so it is dedicated to her. The buttercream and ganache may be made up to one month ahead and frozen; defrost in the refrigerator overnight. The cake may be made one day before assembling.

Makes one 9-inch round cake; serves 12 to 14

1 recipe Quick 'n' Easy Chocolate Cake (page 31), made with coffee instead of water, baked and cooled

1 standard batch Italian Meringue Buttercream, Espresso Variation (page 44)

1½ tablespoons Kahlúa coffee liqueur

One 8-ounce package Heath Bits 'O Brickle Toffee Bits

1 cup miniature semisweet chocolate morsels

½ cup Chocolate Ganache Glaze and Frosting (page 49)

Pastry bag

Large star decorating tip such as Wilton #2110 or Ateco #835

1. Have the cake layers and buttercream ready to use. Use a silicone brush to brush the cake layers with the Kahlúa. Toss together the toffee bits and chocolate morsels in a small bowl; set aside.

2. Fill and frost the cake with buttercream. (Make sure cake is on a cardboard round, as it will make the next step easier.)

3. To apply the toffee bit–morsel mixture: Pick up the cake on the cardboard and hold it over the bowl of morsel mixture with one hand. Apply morsel mixture with other hand, pressing it to the sides of the cake, covering it completely.

4. Use the star tip to make a complete ring of buttercream shells or rosettes around the top outer edge of the cake; it is very important that you make a full ring of large, tall shapes to hold in the ganache that will be poured on top later (see photo). Chill the cake until the buttercream is firm, at least 2 hours.

5. Have the ganache fluid, but not hot. Pour it over the center top of the cake and flood the entire top within the boundaries of the decorative frosting rim; a small, offset icing spatula works very well here to help push the ganache up against the border. Chill the cake until the ganache is firm, at least 2 hours. Bring to room temperature before serving. The cake may be served immediately, or refrigerated overnight in a covered container.

No-Guilt Chocolate Angel Food Cake

Adding cocoa to the batter and drizzling the cake with a chocolate glaze makes this version a tad richer than its classic (nonchocolate) namesake. The glaze is low in calories but tastes exceptionally rich. When preparing the glaze, the water should be as hot as can be from the tap (no need to heat it on the stovetop). Superfine sugar can be purchased at the supermarket, or spin granulated sugar in the food processor until fine.

Makes one 10-inch cake;
serves 12 to 14

Cake

¼ cup Dutch-processed cocoa

3 tablespoons hot water

1 teaspoon vanilla extract

1 cup sifted cake flour

¾ cup sifted confectioners' sugar

Pinch of salt

14 large egg whites, at room temperature

2 teaspoons cream of tartar

⅔ cup superfine sugar

Glaze

1 cup sifted confectioners' sugar

¼ cup Dutch-processed cocoa

3 tablespoons hot water

½ teaspoon vanilla extract

1. To make the cake: Position a rack in the middle of the oven. Preheat the oven to 350°F. You will need a 10-inch, two-piece (loose-bottom) tube pan; leave it ungreased.

2. Combine the cocoa and hot water in a small bowl and stir until smooth. Stir in the vanilla; set aside.

3. Whisk together the flour, confectioners' sugar, and salt in a medium-size bowl to combine and aerate; set aside.

4. In a large bowl, beat the egg whites with an electric mixer on medium-high speed until frothy. Add the cream of tartar and continue to beat until soft peaks form. Gradually add the superfine sugar and continue beating until stiff, but not dry, peaks form.

5. Sprinkle about one-third of the flour mixture over the egg whites and begin to combine by hand using a large balloon whisk. Add half of the chocolate mixture, continue folding with the whisk, then another third of the dry mixture, then the remaining chocolate mixture, and end with the flour mixture. Keep folding with the whisk until well combined, taking care not to deflate the batter. Finish off with a large rubber spatula, if necessary. Carefully spoon the mixture into the tube pan, smoothing the top with a small offset spatula.

6. Bake for 30 to 40 minutes, or until a wooden skewer inserted into the cake comes out clean. Remove the cake from the oven and immediately prop the cake pan upside down on the neck of a thin bottle to cool completely. (Don't worry; the cake won't fall out.) Run an icing spatula around the sides of the

cake. Apply pressure out toward the pan, not in toward the cake, or you might accidentally shave off some of the cake's sides. Turn over to unmold and place on a serving platter. The flat bottom of the cake is now the top. The cake is ready to glaze. Alternatively, the unglazed cake be placed on a cardboard round and double-wrapped in plastic wrap. Store at room temperature and assemble within 24 hours.

7. To make the glaze: Whisk together the sugar, cocoa, hot water, and vanilla in a small bowl until smooth. Scrape into a measuring cup with a spout and slowly pour the glaze all over the cake in a decorative pattern. Allow the glaze to set, about 15 minutes. The cake may be served immediately, or stored at room temperature overnight in a covered container.

The Office Birthday Cake

When a cake is needed at the office for a birthday, baby shower, or farewell party, you need one that feeds many and can be transported easily. I like carrot cakes for this purpose as they are crowd pleasers—plus, with the addition of extra fruit and nuts, this cake will help stave off any midafternoon slump. So that you don't have to worry about losing a good cake pan at the office, this cake is baked in a disposable pan with a snap-on cover. To gild the lily, the cream cheese frosting has the addition of juicy, sweet pineapple. Due to the size of the cake, read the recipe through before starting, as there are some steps that differ from those in the basic carrot cake recipe it is based upon.

Makes one 13 x 9-inch cake; serves 24 to 35

1 disposable aluminum 13 × 9-inch baking pan with snap-on plastic cover

1 recipe batter for Carrot Cake (page 36) using only ½ cup dark raisins and ⅔ cup toasted walnuts halves, chopped

⅓ cup chopped dried cranberries

⅓ cup golden raisins

⅔ cup toasted pecan halves, chopped

Frosting

1 pound full-fat cream cheese, at room temperature, cut into pieces

½ cup (1 stick) unsalted butter, at room temperature, cut into pieces

2½ cups sifted confectioners' sugar

1 cup very well-drained crushed pineapple

1. Position a rack in the middle of the oven. Preheat the oven to 325ºF. Coat the inside of the pan with nonstick cooking spray. Place the pan on a jellyroll pan for support (disposable pans can bend).

2. Prepare the carrot cake according to the directions but combine the orange juice in the recipe with the dark raisins, cranberries, and golden raisins and plump them as directed (there is enough liquid for the dried fruit). Add both the walnuts and pecans when nuts are called for in recipe. Proceed with the recipe as directed.

3. Bake for 1 hour to 1 hour and 5 minutes, or until a toothpick inserted into the cake shows a few moist crumbs when removed. Cool the pan completely on a wire rack. The cake is ready to frost. Or cover the cake with plastic wrap, store at room temperature, and frost within 24 hours.

4. To make the frosting: Place the cream cheese in the bowl of a stand mixer and beat on high speed with the flat paddle until it begins to smooth out. Add the butter and beat on high speed until very smooth, scraping down the bowl once or twice. Add half the sugar and beat on low speed until absorbed, then add the remaining sugar and beat until completely smooth. Beat in the pineapple. The frosting is ready to use and should be applied immediately.

5. Cover the entire top of the cake with the frosting and decorate as desired. The cake may be served immediately, or refrigerated overnight with the cover snapped into place. Bring to room temperature before serving.

In addition to the pan suggested above, this recipe will fill two quarter-sheet pans that measure 12¼ × 8 × 1¼ inches. They are usually sold two to a package with snap-on lids. Because the pans are shallow, the cakes will bake in 20 to 30 minutes. To serve up to 60 people, and if you don't mind the informality of a thinner cake, go this route.

Orange Chiffon Cake with Rose Petals

Chiffon cakes are often baked in angel food cake pans, so they look quite similar. Chiffon cakes, however, use egg yolks, and often include extra egg whites and a bit of oil, which makes for a springy, light cake with a bit more substance than angel food. Once baked, the cake is covered with whipped cream and then showered with edible rose petals. Make sure to buy unsprayed roses, best found at farmer's markets.

Makes one 10-inch cake; serves 12 to 14

Cake

2¼ cups sifted cake flour

1½ cups superfine sugar

2½ teaspoons baking powder

¼ teaspoon salt

6 large eggs, separated and at room temperature, plus 3 additional large egg whites, at room temperature

½ cup vegetable oil such as canola or safflower

¾ cup fresh squeezed orange juice

2 tablespoons finely grated orange zest

1 teaspoon vanilla extract

1 teaspoon cream of tartar

1 recipe Whipped Cream Frosting (page 52)

Fresh unsprayed roses

1. To make the cake: Position a rack in the middle of the oven. Preheat the oven to 325°F. You will need a 10-inch two-piece (loose-bottom) tube pan; leave it ungreased.

2. In a large bowl, with an electric mixer on low-medium speed, combine the flour, 1¼ cups of the sugar, the baking powder, and salt. Make a well in the center of the dry ingredients and add the egg yolks, oil, juice, zest, and vanilla; beat for about 2 minutes on medium speed until smooth.

3. In a clean, grease-free bowl, with an electric mixer with clean beaters on low-medium speed, beat the egg whites until frothy. Add the cream of tartar and beat on high speed until soft peaks forms. Slowly add the remaining ¼ cup sugar and beat until stiff, but not dry, peaks form. Fold the egg whites into the batter just until blended. Scrape into the pan and smooth the top with an offset spatula.

4. Bake for 50 minutes to 1 hour, or until a wooden skewer comes out clean. The top will spring back when lightly pressed. Remove the cake from the oven and immediately prop the cake pan upside down on the neck of a thin bottle to cool completely. (Don't worry; the cake won't fall out.) Run an icing spatula around the sides of the cake. Apply pressure out toward the pan, not in toward the cake, or you might accidentally shave off some of the cake's

Recipe continues on page 126

sides. Turn over to unmold and place on a serving platter. The flat bottom of the cake is now the top. The cake is ready to frost, decorate, and serve. Alternatively, place on a cardboard round and double-wrap in plastic wrap; store at room temperature if assembling within 24 hours.

5. Have the frosting ready to use. Cover the entire cake, top, sides, and inside the center with frosting. Make attractive but casual swirls here and there all over the cake with an icing spatula or the back of a spoon. The cake may be served immediately, or refrigerated overnight in a covered container. Scatter rose petals over the cake right before serving.

P.B.C.B. Cake

This cake appeals to the kid in all of us with flavors of peanut butter, chocolate, and bananas stacked into one. The two cake layers are sliced in half horizontally before being filled and frosted with a milk chocolate–peanut butter frosting, resulting in a tall four-layer cake that serves up to 14 guests.

Makes one 8-inch round cake; serves 12 to 14

Cake

1½ cups all-purpose flour

½ cup Dutch-processed cocoa

1½ teaspoons baking powder

1 teaspoon soda

½ teaspoon salt

½ cup (1 stick) unsalted butter, at room temperature, cut into pieces

1 cup lightly packed light brown sugar

½ cup creamy peanut butter such as Skippy; do not use natural

2 ounces semisweet chocolate, melted

1 large ripe banana, sliced into ½-inch rounds

1½ teaspoons vanilla extract

3 large eggs, at room temperature

⅔ cups buttermilk (preferably low-fat), at room temperature

1. To make the cake: Position a rack in the middle of the oven. Preheat the oven to 350°F. Coat the insides of two 8 × 2-inch round cake pans with nonstick cooking spray, line the bottoms with parchment rounds, then spray the parchment.

2. Whisk together the flour, cocoa, baking powder, baking soda, and salt in a medium-size bowl to combine and aerate; set aside.

3. In a large bowl, with an electric mixer on medium-high speed, beat the butter until creamy, about 2 minutes. Add the sugar gradually and beat until very light and fluffy, about 3 minutes. Beat in the peanut butter, scraping down bowl once or twice. Beat in the chocolate, banana, and vanilla until blended.

4. Beat in the eggs one at a time, scraping down after each addition and allowing each egg to be absorbed before continuing. Add the flour mixture in three additions, alternately with the buttermilk. Begin and end with the flour and beat briefly until smooth. Divide the thick batter evenly between the pans and smooth the tops with an offset spatula.

5. Bake for 25 to 35 minutes, or until a toothpick inserted into the layers shows a few moist crumbs when removed. Cool the pans on wire racks for 8 to 10 minutes. Unmold, peel off the parchment, and place the layers directly on the racks to cool completely. The layers are ready to fill and frost. Alternatively, place the layers on cardboard rounds and double-wrap in plastic wrap; store at room temperature and assemble within 24 hours.

Recipe continues on page 128

Frosting

12 ounces milk chocolate, finely chopped

1 cup (2 sticks) unsalted butter, at room temperature, cut into pieces

3⅓ cups sifted confectioners' sugar (plus extra as needed)

2½ cups creamy peanut butter such as Skippy; do not use natural

¼ cup whole milk, at room temperature (plus extra as needed)

6. To make the frosting: Melt the chocolate and butter together in top of a double boiler or in the microwave; cool slightly. In a large bowl, with an electric mixer on medium-high speed, beat the confectioners' sugar, peanut butter, and chocolate-butter mixture until beginning to come together. Drizzle in the milk and continue beating until creamy and smooth, about 2 minutes. (If frosting is too thick, add more milk; if too thin, add more confectioners' sugar.) The frosting is ready to use.

7. Using a thin, long-bladed knife, horizontally slice each layer evenly in half so there are four layers. Fill and frost with the frosting and decorate as desired. The cake may be served immediately, or stored at room temperature overnight in a covered container.

Polka Dots and Cupcakes Birthday Cake

This bright, colorful cake was inspired by a giant cupcake featured in Pretty Cakes *(Harper & Row, 1986) and a photo of another cake crowned with a tower of mini cupcakes. Years after I first saw the latter photo, I had the good fortune of meeting the food stylist who designed it, Karen Tack, whom I then had the pleasure of working with. In the spirit of "more is better, especially on birthdays," I decided to combine both designs. Take care to make very small pleats for the giant cupcake wrapper (or the scale will not be right) and apply the frosting to the large cake as directed to create the angled sides so that it looks like a cupcake. Also, do not cut the glassine paper before the large cake is filled and frosted as you need to measure its finished, frosted height. A large serving platter allows you to arrange the extra cupcakes around the base of the giant one. This cake does take time and patience, so plan accordingly.*

Makes one 8-inch round cake plus 6 standard and 12 mini cupcakes; serves 18 to 20

1½ recipes batter for Quick 'n' Easy Yellow Cake (page 29)

6 standard size paper liners (Wilton Snappy Stripes Baking Cups or your choice)

12 miniature size paper liners (Wilton Snappy Stripes Baking Cups or your choice)

8-inch cardboard round

1½ recipes Confectioners' Sugar Frosting (page 40)

2 pieces hot pink glassine paper, 24 × 3 to 4 inches each (see Baker's Tip)

Wooden toothpicks

Gel or paste food coloring in pink, orange, and yellow (or colors coordinated with the baking wrappers and glassine)

Pastry bag and coupler

Small round tip such as Ateco or Wilton #3

1. Position a rack in the middle of the oven. Preheat the oven to 350°F. Coat the insides of two 8 × 2-inch round cake pans with nonstick cooking spray, line the bottoms with parchment rounds, then spray the parchment. Line a 6-cup standard muffin tin and a 12-cup mini muffin tin with the appropriate paper liners.

2. Fill the cupcake liners about three-quarters full with batter and bake until a toothpick inserted into a cupcake shows a few moist crumbs when removed, 15 to 20 minutes for standard and 12 to 15 minutes for minis.

3. Divide the remaining batter between the 8-inch pans and bake until a toothpick inserted into the layers shows a few moist crumbs when removed, 25 to 35 minutes.

4. Cool the muffin tins on a wire rack for 6 to 8 minutes, then unmold the cupcakes directly onto the rack. Cool the cake layers for 8 to 10 minutes, then unmold and place directly on the rack to cool completely.

5. Using an 8-inch cardboard round as a base, fill and frost the 8-inch layers with plain white frosting. Build up the frosting along the upper half of the sides so that the cake angles out, creating a classic cupcake shape (see photo). This is best accomplished by adding extra buttercream to the upper area and angling the icing spatula to sculpt the desired shape. Place on a serving platter and measure the height of the cake's side. Cut two 24-inch strips of glassine paper to that height minus ⅛ inch. Beginning at the short ends, fold the paper into ¼-inch accordion pleats. Tape the two pieces together, one short end to another. Line up the long edge of the pleated paper with the bottom edge of the cake and wrap it around the cake, pressing gently to adhere and trimming to fit the circumference. If the frosting is still soft it might hold the paper in place, but I suggest inserting a few toothpicks here and there near the base of the paper, like push-pins (remember to remove them before serving).

6. Tint 1½ cups frosting hot pink and frost the standard cupcakes; set aside (there will be frosting left over). Tint 1 cup frosting vivid orange and frost 11 of the mini cupcakes; set aside (there will be frosting left over). Tint

¼ cup frosting bright yellow and frost the remaining mini cupcake; set aside (there will be frosting left over).

7. Center four standard cupcakes on top of the cake. On top of those, place one orange-topped cupcake in the middle and then arrange a ring of five orange-topped mini cupcakes around it; the center one might be slightly lower, which is okay. Crown the very top of the pile with the yellow cupcake. Extra mini cupcakes can be placed here and there around the cake base. Serve the 2 extra standard cupcakes separately.

8. Fill the pastry bag fitted with a coupler and tip with the remaining yellow frosting. Using the photo as inspiration, apply small dots here and there all over the large base cake. Switch to orange frosting and apply medium-size dots, and then large dots with the pink. The cake may be served immediately, or stored at room temperature overnight in a covered container (if you have one tall enough—try an overturned stockpot).

Baker's Tip I used a color scheme of pink, orange, and yellow, but feel free to use colors of the birthday person's choice. The specific information above is about the cupcake wrappers in the photo; you can use others to suit the décor. The glassine paper used for the giant cupcake is food safe and greaseproof. It can be found at craft stores; look for Martha Stewart's Crafts Glassine Paper. The pleating of the paper is an important, if time-consuming, step. The neater and more even the pleats, the more realistic and attractive the final result.

Pretty-in-Pink Cake

This is a pink cake, inside and out, for anyone who adores pink. Raspberries folded into the basic White Cake batter add flavor, a delicate pink color (especially if frozen rasperries are used), and moistness. The raspberries added to the buttercream yield a bright pink hue; it looks striking with pink candles set into additional whole raspberries ringing the cake. For this decoration, the berries must be very fresh, firm, and dry. Place the desired number of berries, open end up, on the room-temperature cake (the soft buttercream will hold the berries). Insert candles into the openings in the berries and press through into the cake. This should be done right before serving so the berries don't bleed onto the frosting.

Makes one 9-inch round cake; serves 10 to 12

1 recipe batter for White Cake (page 32)

1½ cups fresh or frozen (defrosted and drained) raspberries

1 standard batch Italian Meringue Buttercream, Raspberry Variation (page 44)

Fresh, dry, whole raspberries (same number as candles, optional)

Pink or red candles (optional)

1. Position a rack in the middle of the oven. Preheat the oven to 350°F. Fold 1½ cups raspberries into the prepared batter. Proceed with the recipe as directed.

2. Bake for 30 to 40 minutes, or until a toothpick inserted into the layers shows a few moist crumbs when removed. Cool the pans on wire racks for 8 to 10 minutes. Unmold, peel off the parchment, and place the layers directly on the racks to cool completely. The layers are ready to fill and frost. Alternatively, place the layers on cardboard rounds and double-wrap in plastic wrap; store at room temperature and assemble within 24 hours.

3. Have the frosting ready to use. Fill and frost the cake. The cake may be served immediately, or refrigerated overnight in a covered container. Bring to room temperature before serving. Arrange the berries and candles, if using.

Red Velvet Cake with Cooked Vanilla Icing

A lightly flavored chocolate cake tinted red with food coloring has long been a favorite in the southeastern United States. While the red color might have originally developed from the reaction between the acidic buttermilk and vinegar with the cocoa, red food coloring gives it a boost. You may halve the coloring if you like, but know that many traditional recipes use twice as much. The cooked vanilla icing is typical for this cake. It is smooth, buttery, not too sweet—and very easy to make. It also works well with other cakes that need a vanilla frosting, so give it a try.

**Makes one 8-inch round cake;
serves 10 to 12**

Cake

2 cups sifted cake flour

1 tablespoon natural cocoa

2 teaspoons baking soda

½ teaspoon salt

1 cup buttermilk, at room temperature

1 teaspoon apple cider vinegar or distilled white vinegar

½ cup (1 stick) unsalted butter, at room temperature, cut into pieces

1½ cups sugar

1 teaspoon vanilla extract

2 tablespoons red liquid food coloring

2 large eggs, at room temperature

Icing

1½ cups whole milk

¼ cup plus 1½ teaspoons all-purpose flour

1½ cups (3 sticks) unsalted butter, at room temperature, cut into pieces

1½ cups sugar

1½ teaspoons vanilla extract

1. To make the cake: Position a rack in the middle of the oven. Preheat the oven to 350°F. Coat the insides of two 8 × 2-inch round cake pans with nonstick cooking spray, line the bottoms with parchment rounds, then spray the parchment.

2. Whisk together the flour, cocoa, baking soda, and salt in a medium-size bowl to combine and aerate; set aside. In a separate bowl, whisk together the buttermilk and vinegar; set aside.

3. In a large bowl, with an electric mixer on medium-high speed, beat the butter until creamy, about 2 minutes. Add the sugar gradually and beat until very light and fluffy, about 3 minutes, scraping down the bowl once or twice. Beat in the vanilla and red food coloring.

4. Beat in the eggs one at a time, scraping down after each addition and allowing each egg to be absorbed before continuing. Add the flour mixture in three additions, alternately with the buttermilk. Begin and end with the flour and beat briefly until smooth. Divide the batter evenly between the pans.

5. Bake for 30 to 35 minutes, or until a toothpick inserted into the layers shows a few moist crumbs when removed.

The layers will have begun to come away from the sides of the pans. Cool the pans on wire racks for 6 to 8 minutes. Unmold, peel off the parchment, and place the layers directly on the racks to cool completely. The layers are ready to fill and frost. Alternatively, place the layers on cardboard rounds and double-wrap in plastic wrap; store at room temperature if assembling within 24 hours.

6. To make the icing: Whisk together the milk and flour in a small saucepan. Bring to a simmer over medium heat, whisking constantly. Once it simmers, continue whisking and cook 1 to 2 minutes, or until thickened, smooth, and glossy. Remove from the heat and set aside. Stir occasionally until cool.

7. In a medium-size bowl, with an electric mixer on medium-high speed, beat the butter until creamy, about 2 minutes. Add the sugar and beat on high speed until light and fluffy, scraping down the bowl once or twice. Beat in the vanilla. Add the milk-flour mixture and beat until smooth. The icing is ready to use.

8. Fill and frost the cake and decorate as desired. The cake may be served immediately, or stored at room temperature overnight in a covered container.

She's a Doll Cake

The purple color scheme can be changed to your princess's favorite color. The key is to tint the frosting two colors within the same family—one a deep, rich color and the other a lighter pastel. While the directions are lengthy and specific, the decorations are not difficult to make. You do need a Wilton Wonder Mold Kit, which provides you with the ball gown–shaped mold as well as the doll pick (it's a doll from the waist up; from the waist down it is a pick that easily inserts into the cake).

Makes 1 cake; serves 8

Wilton Wonder Mold Kit

9-inch cardboard round

1 recipe batter for White Cake (page 32), Yellow Cake (page 28), or Dark Chocolate Cake (page 30)

1 recipe Confectioners' Sugar Frosting (page 40)

Gel or paste food coloring, violet or color of choice

Two pastry bags with couplers

Ateco or Wilton tips #2, #15, #18, and #45

Thin elastic pony-tail holder matching the doll's hair color

Edible glitter, purple or color of choice

1. Position a rack in the middle of the oven. Preheat the oven to 350°F. Trace the open end of the Wonder Mold pan onto the cardboard round and trim to the correct size; set aside. Assemble the pan according to the instructions that accompany it. Coat the inside of the pan with nonstick cooking spray, then completely dust with flour and shake out the excess. Scrape the batter into the pan. Baking time will depend on which cake you bake, but begin checking at 25 minutes for all of them. Bake until a wooden skewer inserted into the cake shows a few moist crumbs when removed.

2. Cool the pan on a wire rack for 15 minutes. Remove the rod from the center of the cake. Unmold and place the cake directly on the rack to cool completely. The cake is ready to frost. Alternatively, place it on the cardboard and double-wrap in plastic wrap; store at room temperature if assembling within 24 hours.

3. You can leave the cake as is, but with a bit of trimming with a sharp knife, you can create a more elegant shape. Choose the "front" of the gown and gently shave off some of the cake, beginning at the top. (For the doll pictured I shaved a triangle that began at the top front and ended up with a 5-inch-wide bottom.) Insert the doll pick toward the front of the cake, not in the hole in the center. Turn the cake to the side and you will see that the gown now flows out behind her, creating a dramatic line. Also notice that the top rear of the cake is fairly prominent. Gently shave off a bit along the top rear; you want a gently curving line that flows into the skirt itself (see photo).

Recipe continues on page 138

4. Have the frosting ready to use. Affix the cake to the cardboard with a bit of frosting. Affix this board and cake to the serving platter. Tint three-quarters of the frosting a vivid color and the remaining frosting a paler pastel. Cover the entire rear three-quarters of the cake with the darker frosting, leaving the front 5 inches (the trimmed triangle) bare. Use an icing spatula to apply frosting in an up-and-down motion; this will create soft vertical lines that look like draped fabric.

5. Place each frosting in separate pastry bags, each fitted with a coupler. Using the #45 tip and lighter frosting, apply ruffles to the front of the cake, beginning at the center bottom of the triangle and working your way up to the top. Create the ruffled ribbon effect by moving the pastry bag up and down, up and down as you move upwards. Fill the space to the left and right of the first ruffle with more ruffles until the triangle is filled.

6. Place the #18 tip on the bag with darker frosting. Place small rosettes all along the sides of the triangle on the front and along the bottom of the skirt around toward the back. Use the star tip to make another triangle border down the back.

7. Remove the doll and arrange her hair in a dramatic top bun, using the ponytail holder. Apply darker frosting on her body with your fingers or a small icing spatula to create her heart-shaped neckline and bodice. Hold her over an empty bowl and sprinkle glitter all over her bodice, front and back. Gently shake off any excess (glitter in the bowl can be reused). Use the pastry bag with darker frosting and the #15 tip to pipe rosettes around the hair elastic. Insert her back in place. Gently sprinkle glitter along the rear triangle on the dress bordered by the rosettes.

8. Use the pastry bag with lighter frosting and the #2 tip to pipe a choker-style necklace. Clean the tip and affix it to the bag with darker frosting. Pipe tiny dots all over the dark-colored left and right panels of skirt. Voilà! The cake may be served immediately, or stored at room temperature overnight in a covered container (an overturned stockpot works fabulously).

Baker's Tip

There are numerous ways to be creative with this cake. Give your doll earrings, a bracelet, ropes and ropes of pearls—you get the idea. Obviously, the patterns on the skirt and/or the neckline of her bodice can be varied as well. The doll that comes with the kit is a brunette; you can buy blondes or dolls with other skin tones separately.

Sour Cream–White Chocolate Cheesecake with Raspberries

For some, a rich, creamy cheesecake is the birthday cake of choice; this one combines delicate white chocolate with the tang of raspberries. White Chocolate Cream Cheese Frosting allows for traditional birthday cake decoration; it will look just like a classic frosted cake. The raspberry sauce is optional, but the tangy sweetness of the berries cuts the richness of the cake. Although graham crackers are traditional in cheesecake crust, I prefer the flavor of ground-up purchased crisp oatmeal cookies. You can use a springform pan, but loose-bottom pans (see Resources, page 154) are a huge improvement as they seem to leak much less, which is helpful especially when the pan is immersed in a water bath. This cake is a two-day process, but it freezes very well, so you can make it even a month ahead. Full-fat or Neufchâtel cream cheese can be used for the frosting, but use full-fat cream cheese for the cake or it will be too soft to frost easily.

Makes one 9-inch round cake; serves 14 to 16

Crust

1¼ cups crispy oatmeal cookie or graham cracker crumbs

¼ cup (½ stick) unsalted butter, melted

1 tablespoon granulated sugar

Cheesecake

2 pounds full-fat cream cheese, at room temperature, cut into pieces

1¼ cup granulated sugar

2 large eggs, at room temperature

1 tablespoon freshly squeezed lemon juice

1. To make the crust: Position a rack in the middle of the oven. Preheat the oven to 350°F. Coat the inside of a 9 × 3-inch round loose-bottom or spring-form pan with nonstick cooking spray.

2. Place the cookie crumbs, melted butter, and sugar in a bowl and stir to combine. Press the crust evenly over the bottom of the prepared pan. Bake for 12 to 15 minutes, or until just dry to the touch. Place the pan on a wire rack to cool while preparing the filling. Turn the oven down to 325°F.

3. To make the cheesecake: In a large bowl, with an electric mixer on medium-high speed, beat the cream cheese until creamy, about 3 minutes. Add the sugar gradually and beat until very light and fluffy, about 3 minutes, scraping down the bowl once or twice. Beat in the eggs one at a time, scraping down after each addition and allowing each egg to be absorbed before continuing. Beat in the lemon juice and vanilla. Stir in the sour cream by hand until

Recipe continues on page 140

½ teaspoon vanilla extract

1 cup sour cream, at room temperature

Frosting

12 ounces full-fat or Neufchâtel cream cheese, at room temperature, cut into pieces

9 tablespoons (1 stick plus 1 tablespoon) unsalted butter, at room temperature, cut into pieces

10 ounces white chocolate, melted

1 teaspoon vanilla extract

Sauce

Two 12-ounce bags frozen unsweetened raspberries

¼ to ⅓ cup superfine sugar

1 teaspoon freshly squeezed lemon juice

completely incorporated. Wrap the exterior of cooled pan thoroughly with extra-wide aluminum foil. The seams of the pan must be protected from the water bath. Pour the batter over the crust. Place the cheesecake pan in a larger pan and fill with hot water to come halfway up the cheesecake pan (but not over the edge of the foil).

4. Bake for 55 minutes to 1 hour and 5 minutes. The top should not color (although you might get a spot or two of color) and will look dry and smooth, but the cake will still jiggle when you gently shake the pan. Turn off the oven and let the cake sit in the water bath in the oven for 1 hour as it cools. Remove the pan from the water bath and refrigerate the cake overnight, or up to 2 days, before proceeding. (The cake may be well wrapped in plastic wrap at this point—still in the pan to protect it—and frozen for up to 1 month.)

5. To make the frosting: In a large bowl, with an electric mixer on medium-high speed, beat the cream cheese and butter until creamy, about 2 minutes. Add the melted chocolate and beat until very creamy, about 3 minutes, scraping down the bowl once or twice. Beat in the vanilla. The frosting is ready to use.

6. Unmold the cheesecake: Warm an icing spatula under hot running water and shake dry. Run the spatula around the sides of the cake to release it from the pan. Apply pressure out toward the pan, not in toward the cake, or you might accidentally shave off some of the cake's sides. If using a loose-bottom pan, press the bottom up to release. If using a springform, unlock and remove the pan sides. The cake will still be on the round metal bottom of the pan. Affix this pan with some frosting to a cardboard round of the same size. (If you are brave, you can slide an icing spatula under the cheesecake crust, remove the metal bottom, and place the cake directly on the cardboard.) Make sure the cheesecake is very cold when applying the frosting, as it will be firmer and easier to frost. Frost and decorate as desired. Refrigerate at least 4 hours, or overnight, to set frosting.

7. To make the sauce: Defrost the berries completely overnight in the refrigerator, or at room temperature for a few hours. Do not defrost in the microwave, as the heat will cook the fruit and you will lose some of its fresh color and flavor. Strain off and reserve any liquid.

8. Combine the strained berries with ¼ cup superfine sugar and the lemon juice. Taste and adjust the sugar, if necessary. If it is too thick, add some of the reserved liquid. The sauce is ready to use, or may be refrigerated for up to 3 days in an airtight container.

9. Serve slices of the cake cold, with a bit of sauce alongside. Cheesecake is best sliced with a thin-bladed knife dipped in hot water between cuts.

Tantalizing Fruit "Tart" Birthday Cake

Those who enjoy fruit tarts bursting with colorful fruit arranged over rich, luscious pastry cream will be thrilled with this birthday cake. Two layers of vanilla sponge cake are filled with pastry cream, and fresh fruit is arranged on the top just like a tart. Berries, sliced peaches, kiwis, or any assortment of fruit can be used. I prefer a design with an array of the best fruit I can find. A generous amount of fruit is listed so you can select the best specimens as you create.

Makes one 9-inch round cake; serves 8 to 10

1 recipe Hot Milk Sponge Cake, baked and cooled (page 33)

1 recipe Pastry Cream, chilled (page 53)

Fruit Topping

¾ cup apple jelly

2 nectarines, thinly sliced

2 plums, thinly sliced

2 kiwis, peeled and sliced, left whole, halved or quartered

1½ cups raspberries, left whole

4 strawberries, stemmed and thinly sliced vertically

½ cup blackberries, left whole or halved

¼ cup blueberries, left whole

1. Have the cake layer and pastry cream ready to use.

2. To make the glaze for the fruit topping: Place the jelly in a small saucepan and heat over low-medium heat, stirring gently, until fluid. Set aside but keep warm.

3. Using a thin, long-bladed knife, horizontally slice the cake into half. Place the bottom half, cut side up, on a serving platter. Spread the pastry cream evenly over the layer. Top with the second layer, cut side down. Brush a very thin layer of glaze on the top of the cake; it will act as glue for the fruit.

4. Arrange the fruit in whatever pattern you like. You can make concentric circles, quadrants, or a freeform shape, to name a few approaches. It is helpful if the fruit along the outer edge forms a clean border; it looks good and helps the cake cut cleanly. (Consider edging the border with raspberries or blueberries, for instance.)

5. Use a pastry brush to gently brush melted jelly all over the fruit. The jelly creates a glossy look and protects the fruit from drying out. Refrigerate at least 1 hour or up to 6 hours before serving.

Teeny Tiny Milk Chocolate–Orange Cake

Everyone is entitled to a birthday cake even if there are only a few people around to celebrate— party of two, anyone? This 6-inch cake is small, but it's packed with the delectable flavor combination of milk chocolate and orange. If the cake is for adults only, brush the layers with the optional Grand Marnier liqueur. Two 6 × 2-inch round pans are necessary; they can be found at cake-decorating stores or through mail-order (see Resources, page 154).

Makes one 6-inch round cake; serves 6

1¾ cups sifted cake flour

2 teaspoons baking powder

¼ teaspoon salt

3 large egg whites, at room temperature

¾ cup whole milk, at room temperature

½ cup (1 stick) unsalted butter, room temperature, cut into pieces

¾ cups sugar

1 tablespoon finely grated orange zest

1 teaspoon vanilla extract

1 tablespoon Grand Marnier (optional)

1 recipe Milk Chocolate Frosting (page 48)

1. Position a rack in the middle of the oven. Preheat the oven to 350°F. Coat the insides of two 6 × 2-inch round cake pans with nonstick cooking spray, line the bottoms with parchment rounds, then spray the parchment.

2. Whisk together the flour, baking powder, and salt in a medium-size bowl to combine and aerate; set aside. Whisk together the egg whites and milk in a small bowl; set aside.

3. In a large bowl, with an electric mixer on medium-high speed, beat the butter until creamy, about 2 minutes. Add the sugar gradually and beat until very light and fluffy, about 3 minutes, scraping down the bowl once or twice. Beat in the zest and vanilla.

4. Add the flour mixture in three additions, alternately with the egg white–milk mixture. Begin and end with the flour and beat briefly until smooth. Divide the batter evenly between the pans and smooth the tops with an offset spatula.

5. Bake for 20 to 30 minutes, or until a toothpick inserted into the layers shows a few moist crumbs when removed. The layers will be tinged with light golden brown around the edges and top, and will have begun to come away from the sides of the pans. Cool the pans on wire racks for 5 to 10 minutes. Unmold, peel off the parchment, and place the layers directly on the racks to cool

completely. Brush the layers with liqueur, if desired. The layers are ready to fill and frost. Alternatively, place the layers on cardboard rounds and double-wrap in plastic wrap; store at room temperature if assembling within 24 hours.

6. Fill and frost the cake and decorate as desired. The cake may be served immediately, or refrigerated overnight in a covered container. Bring to room temperature before serving.

Tropical Carrot Cake

Carrot cake enthusiasts will beg you to make this cake year round, not just on their birthdays. What makes it so special is the addition of pineapple, macadamia nuts, and a double dose of coconut from flaked coconut and cream of coconut. Even the cream cheese frosting for this large three-layer cake is flavored with cream of coconut. I use Coco Lopez brand (shake the can well before opening); it can be found in supermarkets nationwide. There are no raisins here, but if desired, add one cup golden raisins along with the nuts.

**Makes one 9-inch round cake;
serves 12 to 14**

Cake

2½ cups all-purpose flour

2 teaspoons baking powder

1 teaspoon baking soda

1 teaspoon salt

1 cup vegetable oil such as canola or safflower

1½ cups granulated sugar

¼ cup cream of coconut

4 large eggs, at room temperature

2 teaspoons ground cinnamon

1 teaspoon ground ginger

1 teaspoon vanilla extract

3 cups lightly packed, finely grated carrots (about ¾ pound)

1½ cups sweetened flaked or shredded coconut

1½ cups canned crushed pineapple, drained very well

1 cup toasted unsalted macadamias, whole or halves, chopped

Frosting

1½ pounds full-fat cream cheese, at room temperature, cut into pieces

½ cup (1 stick) unsalted butter, at room temperature, cut into pieces

4 cups sifted confectioners' sugar

¼ cup cream of coconut

1. To make the cake: Position the racks in the upper and lower thirds of the oven (you'll use both racks). Preheat the oven to 350°F. Coat the insides of three 9 × 2-inch round cake pans with nonstick cooking spray, line the bottoms with parchment rounds, then spray the parchment.

2. Whisk together the flour, baking powder, baking soda, and salt in a large bowl to combine and aerate; set aside.

3. Whisk together the oil, sugar, and cream of coconut until well blended in a medium-size bowl. Whisk in the eggs one at a time until absorbed. Whisk in the cinnamon, ginger, and vanilla, then stir in the carrots, coconut, pineapple, and macadamias.

4. Pour the wet ingredients over the dry ones and stir until combined. The batter will be heavy; make sure you combine well and there are no pockets of flour left. Divide the batter evenly among the pans.

5. Bake for 25 to 35 minutes, or until a toothpick inserted into the layers shows a few moist crumbs when removed. Cool the pans on wire racks for 10 to 12 minutes. Unmold, peel off the parchment, and place the layers directly on the racks to cool completely. The layers are ready to fill and frost. Alternatively, place the layers on cardboard rounds and double-wrap in plastic wrap; store at room temperature and assemble within 24 hours.

6. To make the frosting: In a large bowl, with an electric mixer on medium-high speed, beat the cream cheese and butter until creamy, about 2 minutes. Add half the sugar, beating on low speed, until absorbed. Beat in the cream of coconut, then the remaining sugar, and beat until completely smooth. The frosting is ready to use, and best if used immediately.

7. Fill and frost the cake and decorate as desired. The cake may be served immediately, or refrigerated overnight in a covered container. Bring to room temperature before serving.

White Chocolate Extravaganza "Present" Cake

White chocolate is the theme that runs through this trompe l'oeil cake that looks like an exquisitely wrapped gift. The square cake made with white chocolate is "wrapped" in buttercream and then tied with a "bow" made from white chocolate candy plastic. The tinted buttercream contrasts nicely with the differently colored candy ribbon. I used peach-colored buttercream, and the blue sheen on the bow is made with a pearl dust powder (see Resources, page 154), but you can choose whatever colors you like. Use a high-quality white chocolate such as Valrhona Ivoire. To grate the chocolate for the cake batter, start with a hunk and grate on the large holes of a box grater.

Makes one 8-inch square cake; serves 10 to 12

1 recipe batter for White Cake (page 32)

2 ounces grated white chocolate

1 standard batch Italian Meringue Buttercream, White Chocolate Variation (page 44)

Gel or paste food coloring, peach or color of choice

Confectioners' sugar

1 recipe Candy Plastic (page 55) made with white Candy Melts

Pearl dust, blue or color of choice

Vodka

Small artist's brush, preferably ½ inch to 1 inch wide

1. Position a rack in the middle of the oven. Preheat the oven to 350°F. Coat the insides of two 8-inch square cake pans with nonstick cooking spray, line the bottoms with parchment squares, and then spray the parchment. Fold the grated chocolate into the batter. Proceed with the recipe as directed.

2. Bake for 20 to 30 minutes, or until a toothpick inserted into the layers shows a few moist crumbs when removed. Cool the pans on wire racks for 10 minutes. Unmold, peel off the parchment, and place the layers directly on the racks to cool completely. The layers are ready to fill and frost. Alternatively, place the layers on cardboard rounds and double-wrap in plastic wrap; store at room temperature and assemble within 24 hours.

3. Place the buttercream in a bowl and beat with an electric mixer on medium-high speed until smooth. Add ⅛ teaspoon of food coloring at a time and beat until the color is uniform. Keep adding coloring until the frosting is the desired shade. Fill the cake with frosting and frost the exterior as smoothly as possible; place on a serving platter. Chill for at least 2 hours, or until frosting is very firm.

Recipe continues on page 150

4. Dust your hands and work surface with confectioners' sugar. Knead the candy plastic until softened. Roll out on the work surface to about ⅛ inch thick. Use a ruler and sharp knife or pizza cutter to measure out and cut ribbons about 1¼ inches wide and at least 18 inches long. Place about 1 teaspoon of pearl dust in a small bowl. Add a few drops of vodka and stir until it is of paint consistency. Use the brush to paint the ribbons; allow to dry for a few minutes.

5. Place two long ribbons over the cake, crisscrossing at a right angle, with the junction centered (see photo). Trim so that the ends fit cleanly with the bottom edge of the cake.

6. The bow is made in pieces. Using the photo as guidance, form two separate loops and center them over the crisscross. If the loops are soft and falling in on themselves, ball up plastic wrap and tuck it inside each loop for temporary support. You can add more loops if you like for a more elaborate bow. Form a tiny loop for the center of the bow. Create the ribbon ends by taking two lengths of ribbon and cutting the ends as shown in the photograph; tuck one end beneath the loops. Chill the cake for at least 2 hours, or until ribbon has firmed up. The cake may be served immediately, or refrigerated overnight in a covered container. Bring cake to room temperature before serving (remove the plastic wrap balls, if used).

Winter Wonderland Chocolate Peppermint Cake

I feel strongly about celebrating late-December birthdays properly—with birthday cakes. Those whose birthdays fall during the weeks surrounding Christmas often feel cheated, because their special day is overshadowed by the holiday. This cake is just for them. Peppermint flavoring is added to the Quick 'n' Easy Chocolate Cake batter. While it's still warm from the oven, chocolate mints with creamy centers are placed on top of one layer, allowed to melt, and spread to make a minty central layer. Peppermint whipped cream fills and frosts the cake, and a shower of festive red and white peppermint candy crowns the top. The peppermint flavor used in the cake and frosting is not extract. I like Frontier Peppermint Flavor, which is carried at Whole Foods Markets, or Boyajian Peppermint Flavor (see Resources, page 154). Neither is as strong as pure peppermint oil, but they have a much fresher, truer flavor than extract. If you use pure oil or extract, just taste as you go and tailor the strength of mint flavor to your liking.

**Makes one 9-inch round cake;
serves 10 to 12**

Cake

1 recipe batter for Quick 'n' Easy
Chocolate Cake (page 31)

½ teaspoon peppermint flavor

Six 1¾-inch square creamy white
mint–filled chocolate squares (such
as Ghirardelli Dark Chocolate with
White Mint Filling)

Frosting

3 cups heavy cream

¼ cup plus 1 tablespoon
confectioners' sugar

1 teaspoon peppermint flavor

Pastry bag

Large star decorating tip such as
Wilton #2110 or Ateco #835

½ cup crushed red and white hard
peppermint candies

1. To make the cake: Position a rack in the middle of the oven. Preheat the oven to 350°F. Whisk the peppermint flavor into the prepared batter. Proceed with the recipe as directed.

2. Bake for 25 to 35 minutes, or until a toothpick inserted into the layers shows a few moist crumbs when removed. Place the pans on wire racks and immediately place the chocolate mints on one of the layers. Allow to sit for about 5 minutes, or until the mints soften. Use a small offset spatula to spread the mints into an even layer. Cool completely. Make sure the mint layer has resolidified. Unmold, peel off the parchment, and turn the layer with the mints upright so the mints are on top. The layers are ready to fill and frost. Alternatively, place the layers on cardboard rounds and double-wrap in plastic wrap; store at room temperature and assemble within 24 hours.

3. To make the frosting: In a chilled large bowl, with an electric mixer on medium-high speed, whip the cream until it begins to thicken. Add the confectioners' sugar and peppermint flavoring and beat until stiff peaks form. The frosting should be used immediately.

4. Place the chocolate mint layer, facing up, on a serving platter. Cover with a layer of whipped cream. Top with the second cake layer and spread a thick, smooth layer of whipped cream on top. Place the frosting in the pastry bag fitted with the large star tip. Begin at the base of the cake and pipe a column upward toward the top edge of the cake. When you reach the top, bring the tip up, over, and down, now creating a second column as you pipe downwards (see photo). Continue in this manner until all of the sides are covered. Refrigerate at least 1 hour (or overnight) to set frosting.

5. The cake may be served immediately, or refrigerated overnight in a covered container. Scatter crushed peppermint candy on top of the cake just before serving.

Baker's Tip You can use any kind of thin, creamy-centered dark chocolate mints. The actual number of mints is not important; just make sure you cover the entire surface of the cake layer with a single layer of the mints.

Resources

100 Candles

3710 South Alameda Street
Vernon, CA 90058
(866) 611-8686
(323) 846-8686
FAX (323) 846-2560
www.100candles.com

Hundreds of themed candles including flowers, fruits, vegetables, and animals.

Ateco

August Thomsen Corp.
36 Sea Cliff Avenue
Glen Cove, NY 11542
(800) 645-7170
(516) 676-7100
FAX (516) 676-7108
www.atecousa.net

My favorite cake-decorating turntable is made by Ateco (they call it a Revolving Cake Stand). They also make high-quality tips (which are not on their site; just ask for what you want), decorating bags, icing spatulas, food coloring, and other decorating tools.

Baby Heirlooms

6910 South Highland Drive 7
Salt Lake City, UT 84121
(800) 340-8838
FAX (801) 453-8939
www.babyheirlooms.com

Beatrix Potter and Mother Goose–themed pewter candle holders as well as Reed and Barton silverplate animal holders. They make unique baby shower gifts.

Babykakes Inc.

P.O. Box 22952
Baltimore, MD 21203
www.babykakes.com

All sorts of small toys and candles, perfect for decorating cakes. Horses, butterflies, frogs, farm animals, ballerinas, sports themes (even girls and boys individual basketball sets), dinosaurs, cartoon characters, mini hot dogs and pizza slices, and many more.

Beryl's Cake Decorating and Pastry Supplies

P.O. Box 1584
North Springfield, VA 22151
(703) 256-6951
(800) 488-2749
FAX (703) 750-3779
www.beryls.com

My favorite source for baking supplies. Beryl often answers the phone herself, providing personal and professional customer service. Her company sells baking pans in all shapes and sizes, food coloring, gold and silver powders, pastry bags and decorating tips, gum paste cutters, precut cardboard rounds, cake drums, cake decorating turntables, a large selection of cupcake paper liners, books, and more. A printed catalog is available.

Candy Warehouse, Inc.

5314 Third Street
Irwindale, CA 91706-2060
(626) 480-0899
FAX 626-480 0818
www.candywarehouse.com

All kinds of candies to embellish cakes or to use as birthday favors— from cinnamon Red Hots to chocolates, gummy candies of many shapes, candies that look like Lego toys, dozens of lollipops that look great stuck into cakes, and more.

Chocosphere

(877) 99CHOCO
FAX (877) 912-4626
www.chocosphere.com

If you are looking for high-quality chocolate, order from this fabulous mail-order company. They specialize in all my favorite chocolates such as Valrhona, Scharffen Berger, and Callebaut that are great to eat and to use in the baked goods. Owners Joanne and Jerry Kryszek offer excellent personal service and they ship nationwide. Either order through the website or call to place your order.

Crate&Barrel

1860 West Jefferson Avenue
Naperville, IL 60540
(800) 967-6696
www.crateandbarrel.com

Search website for local stores. They carry a large and varied assortment of platters and cake stands—some with dome covers—as well as cake servers.

Home Town Candy.com

331A Robbins Avenue
Ewing, NJ 08638
(215) 392-4343
FAX 215-392-4340
www.hometowncandy.com

A large selection of marzipan animals at very reasonable prices. You'll find dogs, cats, farm animals, wild animals, and sea creatures in different sizes. Check out their other candies, too.

King Arthur Flour
The Baker's Catalogue

P.O. Box 876
Norwich, VT 05055
(800) 827-6836
(802) 649-3881
FAX (802) 649-5359
www.kingarthurflour.com

High-quality flours, extracts, chocolates, scales, measuring cups and spoons, including ones in odd sizes, and more. Printed catalog also available.

KitchenAid

P.O. Box 218
St. Joseph, MI 49085
(800) 541-6390 (small appliances)
(800) 422-1230 (major appliances)
www.kitchenaid.com

Go directly to this website for a complete listing of their high-quality products. All of my recipes were tested in a KitchenAid oven and made with a 5-quart KitchenAid stand mixer. I bought my mixer almost 20 years ago and it is still going strong. A worthwhile investment for any avid baker.

Meadowsweets

173 Kramer Road
Middleburgh, NY 12122
(888) 827-6477
meadows@midtel.com
www.candiedflowers.com

Toni Elling makes the most exquisite crystallized flowers, taking care with each and every bloom to make certain they are perfect. An ideal resource for those who don't want to crystallize their own flowers. Her website features many different cakes decorated in a variety of inspirational ways.

New York Cake and Baking Distributors

56 West 22nd Street
New York, NY 10010
(212) 675-2253
(800) 942-2539
FAX (212) 675-7099
www.nycake.com

This New York institution offers a variety of quality chocolates, food coloring, gold and silver powders, pastry bags and decorating tips, gum paste cutters and tools, cake pans, parchment, precut cardboard rounds, cake decorating turntables—everything necessary for baking and decorating cakes.

Parrish's Cake Decorating Supplies, Inc.

225 West 146th Street
Gardena, CA 90248
(213) 324-2253
(800) 736-8443
FAX (213) 324-8277

Cake pans, decorating equipment, cake decorating turntables, loose-bottom pans, and more.

Sur La Table

Pike Place Market
84 Pine Street
Seattle, WA 98101
(206) 448-2244
(800) 243-0852
www.surlatable.com

Cake pans, high heat–resistant spatulas, measuring cups, Microplane zesters, and fabulous serving platters and pedestals. Call for locations. Printed catalog available.

Sweet Celebrations / Maid of Scandinavia

7009 Washington Avenue South
Edina, MN 55439
(800) 328-6722
(952) 943-1661
(952) 943-1508
FAX (952) 943-1688
www.sweetc.com
www.maidofscandinavia.com

This company offers a huge array of equipment including pastry bags and decorating tips, chocolates, food coloring, candy decorations, precut cardboard rounds, candles, cake decorating turntables, etc. Printed catalog available.

Williams-Sonoma

P.O. Box 7456
San Francisco, CA 94120
(415) 421-4242
(800) 541-2233
FAX (415) 421-5253
www.williams-sonoma.com

Famous for their mail order catalogs and stores nationwide. Well-made, accurate measuring tools, vanilla extract, some chocolate and cocoa, and other baking equipment including pans, Microplane zesters, and spatulas of all sorts.

Wilton Industries, Inc.

2240 West 75th Street
Woodbridge, IL 60517
(630) 963-7100 ext. 4811
(800) 794-5866
FAX (888) 824-9520
www.wilton.com

Great catalog with heavy-duty pans, pastry bags and decorating tips, food coloring, parchment, cupcake paper liners, Candy Melts, candles, a covered cake storage platter, and much more.

Birthday Cakes by Categories

Measurement Equivalents

Please note that all conversions are approximate.

Liquid Conversions			Weight Conversions			Oven Temperatures		
U.S.	Metric		U.S./U.K.	Metric		°F	Gas Mark	°C
1 tsp	5 ml		½ oz	14 g		250	½	120
1 tbs	15 ml		1 oz	28 g		275	1	140
2 tbs	30 ml		1½ oz	43 g		300	2	150
3 tbs	45 ml		2 oz	57 g		325	3	165
¼ cup	60 ml		2½ oz	71 g		350	4	180
⅓ cup	75 ml		3 oz	85 g		375	5	190
⅓ cup + 1 tbs	90 ml		3½ oz	100 g		400	6	200
⅓ cup + 2 tbs	100 ml		4 oz	113 g		425	7	220
½ cup	120 ml		5 oz	142 g		450	8	230
⅔ cup	150 ml		6 oz	170 g		475	9	240
¾ cup	180 ml		7 oz	200 g		500	10	260
¾ cup + 2 tbs	200 ml		8 oz	227 g		550	Broil	290
1 cup	240 ml		9 oz	255 g				
1 cup + 2 tbs	275 ml		10 oz	284 g				
1¼ cups	300 ml		11 oz	312 g				
1⅓ cups	325 ml		12 oz	340 g				
1½ cups	350 ml		13 oz	368 g				
1⅔ cups	375 ml		14 oz	400 g				
1¾ cups	400 ml		15 oz	425 g				
1¾ cups + 2 tbs	450 ml		1 lb	454 g				
2 cups (1 pint)	475 ml							
2½ cups	600 ml							
3 cups	720 ml							
4 cups (1 quart)	945 ml							
(1,000 ml is 1 liter)								

Index

Note: *Italicized* page references indicate photographs.